Poet
Mo

Norwich

Edited by Donna Samworth

First published in Great Britain in 2004 by:
Young Writers
Remus House
Coltsfoot Drive
Peterborough
PE2 9JX
Telephone: 01733 890066
Website: www.youngwriters.co.uk

SB ISBN 1 84460 386 5

Foreword

This year, the Young Writers' 'Poetry In Motion' competition proudly presents a showcase of the best poetic talent selected from over 40,000 up-and-coming writers nationwide.

Young Writers was established in 1991 to promote the reading and writing of poetry within schools and to the youth of today. Our books nurture and inspire confidence in the ability of young writers and provide a snapshot of poems written in schools and at home by budding poets of the future.

The thought effort, imagination and hard work put into each poem impressed us all and the task of selecting poems was a difficult but nevertheless enjoyable experience.

We hope you are as pleased as we are with the final selection and that you and your family continue to be entertained with *Poetry In Motion Norwich* for many years to come.

Contents

The Poems

Tempestuous Night

I'm alone, feeling insecure.
Outside is another world, it seems.
A world of terror and hazards,
The wind is whistling and swirling.

I'm alone, feeling insecure.
Thoughts flashing in my mind,
Of an imaginary monster,
Whose movement and step makes the earth tremble.

I'm alone, feeling insecure.
The constant pounding of the wind,
Banging against my door.
Shaking the locks and hinges.

I'm alone, feeling insecure,
Is there safety in these walls?
At any moment, disaster could strike.
The telephone rings, I know what is coming.

I'm alone, feeling scared and unsafe.
As I struggle outside, battling against the tempest storm.
I can see the whirlwinds of leaves and branches,
Rushing down and battering the ground.

Still alone, I am terrified,
As I trudge through the sodden mud,
I can see the sky, darkened with storm clouds,
A great roaring torrent of air is encompassing me.

I am alone, petrified,
Clinging on for my life.
Hit by debris and bleeding,
I feel as if the life within me is coming to an end.

Tim Creak (14)
Acle High School

Tempest

The house is quivering,
The horizon is ablaze
With the setting sun
And the trees are striding through the darkness.

Thunder is rolling,
Ending in crashes
That shatter the windows
And rattle the doors.

Lightning pierces
Huge grey clouds
And lights up patches
Of whistling grass.

Trees arched and shaking
Are silhouetted against an angry sky
And crying out over the barren land,
The walls are tickled by the wind.

Out at sea the wooden shack
Is battered by invisible hands
And is lit up by
A smouldering light.

Freya Darrell Hewins (13)
Acle High School

Scottish Weather

As I sat in the warmth of my cosy cottage,
The heavens battled above me.
Bolts of lightning were getting thrown everywhere.
The wind tapped at my window, growing impatient,
Whilst the trees clashed together like a percussion performance.
Feeling threatened, I headed for the kitchen.
Even the creak of the stairs made me jump out of my skin.

Suddenly, before I turned the kettle on,
The shrill ring of my home phone alarmed me greatly.
I picked it to hear that it was my friend looking for a comfort pal.
Agreeing to it, I didn't know what I was about to face.
I quickly grabbed my keys and raincoat.
The heavens and sky were like cat and dog.
Booming voices of thunder could be heard very distinctively.

The whistling of the wind was ear-piercing as I climbed into the coldness of my almost dead car.
Sticky hands gripped to the wheel,
Making sure I stayed to the road.
The pounding drum in my body almost blocked out the rage of war
Inside my safety shell.
I reached for my destination.
Would I clasp it?

Charlotte Perry (13)
Acle High School

The Game Of The Heavens

I sit by the fire, wrapped in a blanket.
The curtains are drawn
But they can't disguise the storm outside.
I am cosy, while outside I imagine streaks of lightning
Darting across the sky, teasing the heavens.
Thunder, its predator, growls and roars, chasing it,
A heavenly game of tag – cat and mouse.
The rain drums on the house,
Seeking a home for the night.
Swirling, dancing winds –
Encircling the world with a cold grip.
Huddling puddles dispersed by angry traffic,
Animals scurry to safety.
I am thrilled yet apprehensive; sheet lightning illuminates my room
For a split second.
The fire is dying. I struggle closer to make the most of the
Dying embers.
The phone rings. A call out.
Dragging myself away from the fire,
I prepare to do battle with the storm.

Open the door.
Step out into another world.

The sky is playing games,
The earth is merely a toy,
A ball to be tossed lightly around.
Circling winds wrap around me, their prey.
Spitting, biting, gnawing,
Grasping me with their piercing talons,
I am defenceless against the power of the storm.
Soaking, all pervading rain.
I am vulnerable. Another toy in the game. Thunder threatens overhead.

I rush for the safety of the car.

Sara Timms (13)
Acle High School

Wild Outdoors

As I feel safe inside my home,
The storm is raging outside,
Feeling glad that I'm not out there,
I watch out of the window.

The trees frantically blow around,
As the animals return
To their safe and warm hidden homes.
Rain beats upon the window.

When I enter the wild outdoors,
The bright lightning crashes down
And while the strident thunder rumbles,
The wind pushes me around.

The surrounding flash before me,
Whenever the lightning strikes
And so I return to my home,
I now feel safe once again.

Clair Duncan (13)
Acle High School

Storm, Storm, Storm, Storm, Storm

Storm . . . crashing, thundering, destroying, our worst fear
Storm . . . it's coming, growing, crackling, I sit at home, scared
Storm . . . raging, killing, eating, it reaches its peak
Storm . . . falling, thudding, crumpling, the wreckage falls to earth

Storm . . . drying, crying, whimpering, the clouds float away
Storm . . . gone, left, wasteland, I stare at the destruction
Storm . . . flown away, vanished, sun's out, it will not be forgotten.

Seb Fisher (13)
Acle High School

Shakespearean Sonnet

My mum asked me to go down to the shops,
Because we were completely out of bread.
As I walked there I went past fields of hops
And factories all with chimneys made of lead.
When I got to the shops they had run out,
Delivery was not in until next week.
I shouted at them – they went up the spout
And threw at me a cabbage and a leek.
When I got home my mum was really cross,
She said, 'You must stand up for yourself more.'
I was told off for the money I had lost
And spanked 'til I collapsed upon the floor.
I was sent to bed without any tea,
My stomach rumbled through the night - poor me.

Kit Marsden (13)
Acle High School

My Love

My love's eyes are not like the night,
Sugar is far less sweeter than his heart,
Although his temper can get him into a fight,
No goldfish will ever be as smart.
His face is far cuter than a polar bear,
If the best were perfect, then so is my love.
To find someone like him, it is quite rare.
His teeth may be white, but not like a dove.
I love to see him happy, yet he will
Never know how happy he makes me.
If I ever lose him, tears will fill,
I hope not anyway, I will miss thee.

Kerri-Anne Peachment (13)
Acle High School

Bryant Sonnet I

He is my dream and everything I see,
He haunts my thoughts as if he were my king,
My heart is pounding every time I see,
The way he looks at me must be a sin.

His spiky hair reminds me of cold ice,
His skin is dark like a black full moon at night,
His acting is so graceful and precise,
When he enters a dark room it is light.

His smile is warm enough to make me melt,
He makes my heart pound up and down all day,
His smooth skin is as good as silky felt,
His body is perfectly formed each way.

All in all he is the best in the world,
His love to me is like a precious pearl.

Polly Bryant (13)
Acle High School

Sea Of Storms

I watch from the window,
The tides of air that are rising,
As the oak tree falls under the tide,
It becomes seaweed.

The shotgun covered in a shroud of grey,
Fires lead pellets from the sky,
Every now and then I hear the blast of the gun,
Great blinding lines cock the weapon.

The lead from the sky has melted to form bowls of liquid,
The current has bombarded trees with rocks,
Though now the tide is going out,
The sky is tainted with cuts of blue.

Robert Lee (13)
Acle High School

These Things I Want:-

Gold necklaces and diamond rings,
Crystal cherubs wearing wings,
To be a famous movie star with gigantic mansions and flashy cars.
Horses galloping wild and free although they'd all belong to me.
An emerald city just for me,
A river of chocolate, no, make that a sea.
An exotic island with lots of palm trees,
That no one could find except gorgeous men and me.
I want my own theme park with the world's best rides,
Shows and roller coasters, different shapes and sizes.
I'd have builders, cleaners, maids and cooks,
Although none of them could improve my looks.
School would be banned on my demand,
Well that would be on my beautiful land.
Work would never have to be done
Because everyone else would be doing some.
I'd want my own theatre where I could perform,
From dawn to dusk and dusk to dawn.
I'd have my own genie, my dreams would come true,
But not just three wishes to infinity and two.
I'd be my own god and rule the world,
With long locks of hair delicately curled.
A huge widescreen cinema in my living room,
Where I'd watch films all day until I saw the moon.

Even though I know I can't,
These are all the things I want.

Emily Bedwell (13)
Acle High School

Storm

Midnight,
Storm racing outside.
Howling, howling:
Rain a soaking tide.

Phone,
Raising me from my chair,
Ringing, ringing:
Introduction to a nightmare.

Danger,
I have to flee,
Running, running:
Trying hard to see.

Bushes,
Now have eyes,
Watching, watching:
I can hear their cries.

Something,
Springing at me,
Falling, falling:
Nothing there to see.

Safe,
All alone,
Living, living:
Hearing the telephone.

Storm,
Like never before,
Raging, raging:
Beating on my door.

Heather Durrant (13)
Acle High School

The Bridesmaid

Smelling the strong stench of lady's perfume,
The hushed whispers from outside,
But the sound is taken over by my heavy heartbeat
And my deep slow breathing.
The golden ring in my hand
Glinting like the sun outside,
Inside of me, it's not sunny, it's bleak,
Cold and lonely.
Green and yellow closing in on me,
As my dress suffocates me and my nerves.
I cannot do this, how can I get out of this?
The bitter-sweet taste of the orange lingers in my mouth,
Clinging onto my taste buds.
Everyone is expecting me to do this,
But they do not know.
How can I let my sister do this?
How can I be a bridesmaid for her?
How can I let her marry the man I love?

Holly Noon (13)
Acle High School

The Challenge Of Education

Five days out of seven he would meet their morbid tone
He bore, with a drill, the same things into their air-filled heads
His wisdom would outrageously flaunt itself upon their deaf ears
Their eyes were open but not in use
Their backs were straight but longing to be slumped
Their heads held high but dreaming of lost summers
Relentlessly he tried and tried again to conquer
The monumental mountain of knowledge
When finally the signal went
The once docile pupils would scatter like pieces of shrapnel
From an explosion
Then, alone, when the dust settled, the teacher
Fought back the tears and prepared for the next day.

Joseph Small (13)
Acle High School

Stormy Times

Out of my window I hear a tree squeak
A crack and a snap
Then a large smash

The thunder roars
And the lightning flashes
Another bang and a couple more crashes

Got to get out
For the sake of my health
Driving through trees I slip like a stealth

A tree is coming down
I am going to drive under
If I'm not fast enough I will crash like thunder

I got out OK
Now that's a fact
All in one piece, all intact.

Sam Mallett (13)
Acle High School

Andrew's Sonnet

My love's eyes are rich mahogany brown,
Inside are tiny dewdrops, twinkling,
I know he should be wearing a king's crown,
Being his queen would be wishful thinking!
The tips of his spiky hair gleam silver,
Placed on his head like marbled chocolate,
His sweet melting look makes my legs quiver,
His sacred picture is in my locket.
His husky voice makes my hair stand on end,
He calls my mobile just like my best mate,
But when we talk he feels like more than my friend,
I know that my love for him is not faint.
Other girls may not appreciate him
And yet I know my love is light not dim.

Kate Maddison (13)
Acle High School

Midnight Massacre

As the red phoenix gives way to the silver hawk,
The black stallions of night roll on,
With flashing teeth and flowing manes,
They vent their anger on the sky.
Whilst the stampede carries on high above,
The lost spirits of the sky whistle,
Discouraging thoughts through the keyhole,
Wolves hear their cousins and howl to the silver hawk,
She hovers, observing all, still and serene.
The heavens bang out on bass drums,
To add to the chorus of death
And in a split second, the sky is lit by a blinding white light,
Only to be gone in an instant.
The light continues its snake dance,
Only a few go solo,
Striking a rhythmic beat on the earth.
The sea has turned on the land,
Pounding the cliff face with white hands,
Hoping to tear it to pieces.
As the figure steps outside the door,
He is instantly flung into a battle of the elements.
His excitement turns to fear in the midst of it,
A cat howls from underneath a tree,
Brought down by ill-wishers,
Carnage of another kind
And as the wind rules above the clouds,
He sits there now warm and dry,
Waiting for the red phoenix,
To chase the storm away.

Rachel Page (13)
Acle High School

British Weather Strikes Again

I sit in my comfy chair,
That's covered with cat hairs,
Next to the blazing fire,
Time is so slow, it's almost expired.

It is a cold and lonely night,
I can hear dogs barking in fright,
Wind is rocking the outside world,
Trees are swaying and dead leaves whirl.

Rain pattering, roof tiles clattering,
Drains gurgling, thirsty worms surfacing,
Thunder clashes, lightning flashes,
Winds howl and dogs growl.

The phone rings, I have to go,
It's bad news I know,
I put on my coat and open my umbrella,
Good old British weather!

The rain hammers hard,
I get into my car,
I slam the door shut,
The engine goes *phut*.

I sigh and clamber out,
I see kids scream and pout,
I see umbrellas blown inside out,
I see people moan, groan and shout.

I run across the road,
Ignoring the Green Cross Code,
A lorry zooms around the corner and screeches to a halt,
He knocks me down, says it wasn't his fault!

Jess Revill (13)
Acle High School

Raging Storm

Thunder drumming through the clouds,
My heart thumping hard in my chest.
Rain beating down into the mud,
My clothes becoming soaked through.
The eerie creak of the back gate,
Sends a shiver down my spine.
The wind roars through the sky,
Whipping my hair about so I can barely see.

Inside, in front of the warm fire,
Snuggled up with my cat, Felix.
I watch the storm, it seems so gentle.
The thunder rolls around in the clouds,
The rain taps on the windows,
The wind softly whistling through the trees.
I sit there for hours fascinated by the lightning,
Forking across the sky in shades of purple, blue and white.

Jess Marsh (13)
Acle High School

Floodlights Of Glory

Floodlights of glory
Shine on the brave,
Hear the crowd roar
As the keeper makes a save.

The tackle was hard,
Manager's eyes filled with dread,
The ref goes to his pocket
And pulls out a red!

Feel the power,
Smell the fear,
He's done the last man,
The net bursts, the whistle, the cheer.

Arlo Reddick (12)
Earlham High School

The Special

A meeting was held quite far from Earth,
'It's time again for another birth,'
Said the angels to the Lord above,
'This special child will need much love.'

His progress may be very slow,
Accomplishment He may not show
And He'll require extra care,
From the folks he meets down there.

He may not run or laugh or play,
His thoughts may seem so far away,
In many ways He won't adapt
And He'll be known as handicapped.

They will not realise straight away,
The leading role they're asked to play,
But with this child sent from above,
Comes stronger faith and richer love

And soon they'll know the privilege given,
In caring for their gift from Heaven.
Their precious charge so meek and mild,
Is Heaven's very special child.

Leanne Saffer (13)
Earlham High School

Witches

Three-eyed witches sit in gloom,
Wondering if their next victim will come soon,
Stirring their cauldron with a wooden spoon,
Glazing up, peeking at the full moon.
I heard that once they caught a child,
Rumour has it his name was Max Wild!
So keep tucked in bed and out of sight,
So you won't be next, day or night.

Lucy Larkins (13)
Earlham High School

Mum

When you're down and frightened,
Alone and blue,
There will always be
Someone thinking of you.

When you're unsure, upset,
Tired, confused,
I will always be here
To help you through.

Another month,
Another year,
Another smile,
Another tear,

Another winter,
Summer too,
But there'll never be
Another you!

Everyone knows
Life ain't fair,
But when you need me,
I'll be there.

Anytime,
Any place,
Anywhere,
Cos you're one in a million and that's very rare!

Jessy Hall (13)
Earlham High School

A Man Apart

A man apart
A different face
A lonely body needs his space
A breathing place
Defies rat race
Wants only for a state of grace

A man unique
A different soul
Nurtured by old rock 'n' roll
A totem pole
Girls' hearts he stole
A being puzzled by the whole

A man, a boy
A different thought
A tidal wave in which he's caught
He won't be bought
His friendship's sought
Yet he's the one who is distraught

A human boy
A different rhyme
He's walking forward all the time
A slippery climb
A guitar's chime.

Ntobeko Ndiweni (13)
Earlham High School

A Footy Poem

Sitting on the sideline, looking at the pitch,
Number three gets tackled by a little titch,
Ref blows his whistle, on goes me,
I go on and off comes three.
45 minutes to go, 3-0 down,
Captain's angry, shows a little frown,
We want a win, have to score,
But it's OK if we get a draw.
I set up our first goal, it was a smacker,
I was in the second, it was a cracker,
10 minutes to go, 3-2 was the score,
I scored the third to make it a draw.
I ran in the area, a man tackles me mentally,
I go flying and win a penalty,
I gaze at the keeper, dripping with sweat,
I hit the ball in the back of the net.
Final whistle goes, we win the game,
We win the league and the cup is the same!

Michael Cullum (13)
Earlham High School

Amber!

Amber, Amber everywhere,
Her scary face and scary hair,
She annoys me nearly every day,
I never know just what to say.
She smacks her ruler on her leg,
Pretending that it is my head,
She nicks my money for my lunch,
If I have none, I get a punch,
Oh wait, oh look, here she comes,
Blinking her eyes and shaking her bum!

Jazmine Shalders (12)
Earlham High School

My Views Of The World

Man strives to reach the moon
To land on Mars,
To explore the stars,
Maybe too soon.

Who's exploring the Earth?
To cure the wars,
To cure the hunger,
What are we worth?

Millions of people dying,
Children crying,
Women weeping,
Desperate for help, who is paying?

Maybe some day soon,
The government will think,
To love and cherish,
To bring peace and forget the moon.

Pippa Glanfield (12)
Earlham High School

Love

I love you more than I love myself,
Not a day goes by without thinking of you,
You may not be rich but that's okay,
Because that first little nibble makes me anxious for more,
Wherever you come from is cool with me,
'Cause as long as I'm with you, you light up my life,
You come in all shapes and sizes,
But I like you best when you're a *lion.*

Anna Eastwick (13)
Earlham High School

I Have This Feeling

I have this feeling about someone,
But I don't know how she feels,
When I see her, my heart rate goes up,
I just can't stop smiling, but why?

I have this feeling inside me,
I don't like to think about it,
I just don't want it to be love,
But what else can it be?

I have this feeling about someone,
She is so far but she feels like she's right here,
I just feel like I can jump an ocean.

I have this feeling inside me,
That she will not want me,
She will never say yes to me,
She cannot possibly like me, or will she?

All I need to do in time of need is remember her face,
Remember her, imagine her there, then I can do anything,
She inspires me to do so much, so I feel I can do anything,
So I wrote this.

Bilal Khurram (13)
Earlham High School

Shopping

S hopping is the thing for me,
H eavy bags are what I need,
O pening early, closing late,
P layboy, I can hardly wait.
P rada is the next big thing,
I n any season, even spring,
N ow for the final words of fashion,
G ucci, Gucci, Gucci.

Robyn Freeman (13)
Earlham High School

Heroes

Right in front of them,
The building stood burning,
As the people stood,
Silently staring.

The deafening noise
Of crashing beams,
Was hardly enough
To silence the screams.

Entering the inferno,
The firemen scurried,
Through the narrow corridor,
Where a young boy was buried.

Shielding their ears
From the thundering sound
Of falling metal
And bricks all around.

Dashing through the flames,
With incredible speed,
Rushing to those trapped
And need to be freed.

Dodging the glass,
Which fell like knives,
In a desperate attempt
To save those lives . . .

Glenn Stanton (14)
Earlham High School

Flying High

Flying high in the midnight sky
Up into outer space
Into a perfect world of such
Wonderful grace

Flying high in the midnight sky
Trying to reach the burning sun
Like a passionate love
You'd give to one

Flying high in the midnight sky
Trying to reach the glowing moon
If you listen hard enough
You'll hear its lullaby tune

Flying high in the midnight sky
Try to reach a diamond-like star
That seems so near
But so far

Flying high in the midnight sky
Passing the planets perfectly aligned
The atmosphere all around you
Will totally blow your mind

Flying high in the midnight sky
Up into outer space
Into a perfect world
Of such wonderful grace.

Kyle Dmoré (14)
Earlham High School

I'm Running Through The Trenches

I'm running through the trenches,
I start to question why,
I'm running through the trenches,
A man gives out a cry,
I'm running through the trenches,
I see my friend get shot,
I'm running through the trenches,
My stomach is a knot,
I'm running through the trenches,
The ground begins to shake,
I'm running through the trenches,
My body starts to quake,
I'm running through the trenches,
The bangs deafen my ears,
I'm running through the trenches,
I'm drowning in my fears.

Billy Blackwood (13)
Earlham High School

Love

Love is a feeling that grows in the heart,
Love can be strong and so can it be weak,
If people are in love, they will not part,
If love is so strong it can't reach its peak.
Feelings can be expressed in many ways,
All different ages can all be in love,
Even between children and even gays,
Love is as beautiful as two white doves.
Love can be broken causing so much pain,
When there is no love, people tend to hurt,
Families are all in a loveable chain,
This makes many people feel like dirt.
This feeling will keep partners together,
Love is so strong, it can last forever.

Matthew Fairweather (15)
Earlham High School

Horror

Dusky, it was like night-time,
Faint cries all around me,
Tall buildings on fire,
Dim remains of the planes falling everywhere.
Blackness has taken over,
Writhing bodies hanging out of windows,
Fear takes me over,
Mystery taking its toll.
Solitude, I started to run away,
Desolation in motion,
Unendurable pain as I see two buildings on fire.
Dead people lay outside the towers,
Stillness as I stare,
Gaunt walls are all that remain,
Spectrally gazing like a telescope, I stand in dismay.
The lifeless windows like fingernails,
My imagination was in stillness,
Terror as I saw people jump out of the windows,
Horror as the buildings collapsed.
Contorted shapes lay on the road,
Erect concrete lay everywhere,
Motionless I stood, staring at the remains,
Disaster is all around me.
A stillness, it feels like there are ghosts all around me,
A sense of doom lay everywhere,
Pitchy blackness has taken over the world,
Why?

Robert Marshall-Nichols (13)
Earlham High School

It's A Small World

The corridor was vast and endless.
The walls were plain and colourless.
This place seemed so fake and artificial.

The large structure ahead seemed so daunting.
We got closer and it got bigger.
This was the vessel to take us to a place where normal life
Ceased to exist.
The ladder, which accessed the monumental structure, was gigantic.
We entered the vessel and everything seemed so plain.
Yet the technology seemed to be from another world.

Time seemed to be in fast-forward from the moment we entered.
Five, the countdown had started.
Four, we were finally going.
Three, this was the moment we had always been waiting for.
Two, seconds away from the permanently starry night sky.
One, we braced ourselves as the engines roared furiously.

Our faces seemed crushed under the pressure.
My heart pounded madly.
The light was getting brighter,
Then all of a sudden, everything went pitch-*black*.

Shannon Goldsmith (14)
Earlham High School

My Poem

Someone, you are my one true love
You must have fallen from the sky above
Heaven is not a place for you neither is Hell
The one true place for you to be would be in my wishing well.

Byron James (13)
Earlham High School

Far Away

Did you see me? Head up high
Walking strong, eye to eye
My life was not so bitter then
But it changed so suddenly
For all this time I was alive
It seems to have been this moment in time
The one thing to have changed it all
Was the way it turned so cold!

But this one light
In the sky
Was the thing that I passed by
I should have stayed
And watched it fall
Did it ever hurt before?
How ever bright the future is
You should always try to exist
With a word to help you along
Never hold back and please be strong

To the end of all this pain
And all the sorrow you have in your heart
Just remember that all can change
If the past is never too far
But just next time watch your back
For the problems you will lack
Not every day will be the same
For every person will live again

Far away I'm on my own
Don't know where to turn to anymore
Is this place the last resort
Or has the future become too sore?

Terri Jones (14)
Earlham High School

Oh Why Won't Love Be Mine?

I sit alone,
Waiting for a call.
Waiting for my love to spring,
I hope it will be soon,
As loneliness is killing me
And shivering down my spine.
Hoping to be happy again,
Oh why won't love be mine?

I sit and hope it will be soon,
Cold and lonely, I begin to sleep,
As something wakens me,
Loud and a chime,
I wake up and I begin to jump,
It went quiet and I'm alone again,
I sit there staring at the time,
Oh why won't love be mine?

Sophie Jay (12)
Earlham High School

What Is Love?

Love is many things,
We don't know what it means,
Love, love everywhere,
Can you help me? What does it mean?
Love is a thing,
In many ways,
We hear songs about love,
But we can never understand them,
Love can mean anything to us,
Adults don't tell us,
Love is all around us
And that is why we are here.

Zoe Arnold (13)
Earlham High School

My Cat, Milly

I have a cat called Milly,
She acts very silly,
She pounces on all the cats,
Who lay asleep on mats,
She goes out in the morning
And won't come back until Mum's snoring,
When she comes back,
She'll sleep in her sack,
When she wakes up in the morning,
She won't stop yawning,
She laps up her milk,
To make her fur as soft as silk,
She watches the telly,
As she lays on her belly,
She tries to run up the walls,
But every time she falls,
I have a cat called Milly,
Now do you believe she's silly?

Samantha Durrant (13)
Earlham High School

Football Crazy

Fans are roaring in the crowd
Liverpool fans are shouting loud
Man U's keeper's let one in
The crowd's roar becomes a din

We're back into the second half
Giggs has gone down, holding his calf
It's getting towards the end of the game
Man U are losing, oh the shame

Liverpool won, what sure bliss
I wish I could play football like this.

Terri Gray (13)
Earlham High School

Evil

Evil, evil brews among us, exploding,
Bubbling and screaming,
All of this from evil.
Evil is a horrifying thing,
Everybody knows, evil everywhere.
People say there is definition for evil,
Except fear, I'm telling you now,
Evil is the worst word there is.
People run from evil,
Others stand and stare,
You never know when evil is brewing,
So beware, evil is a nightmare.
Stand and stare at evil eyes,
You never know when people pounce,
So be on your guard,
Make sure you don't pounce yourself.

Jake Grady (12)
Earlham High School

The Dream

As she was walking down the street
She stopped and looked
She saw disturbing things in the little street
Butchers not cutting meat
Bakers not baking bread
The strangest thing of all, it was as silent as the dead
She walked on very cautiously
Stopping sometimes to look
She felt as if she was hanging off a cliff
Like a perch on a hook
She could finally see her door
Gloomy in the rain
She almost touched the golden knob
Then suddenly she woke.

Samantha Tidd (11)
Earlham High School

A Storm Of Anger And Innocents!

Inside of me something is happening
Something strange and horrid

Anger is forming like a fierce storm
I want to take my feelings out on someone
Or something but of course I can't

It's getting bigger, growling slowly
I can't describe the feeling anymore

Lately I have had weird emotions
Sometimes I'm happy, sad and worried
But why do these things which seem like curses
Have to pick on me?

I'm innocent, I really am
I wouldn't hurt a fly
They think I killed her
How could they think that of me?

Keri-Anne Innes (12)
Earlham High School

First Love, Romeo And Juliet

I am stuck in a box, I cannot escape,
I love him yet I'm supposed to hate him,
My fear for his safety is immeasurable,
I cannot live on like this,
Why can't we be together?
I want to know,
It's our destiny,
It's our love,
Which can never be undivided.
We'll be together,
Always and forever,
Amen.

Jake Hursey (13)
Earlham High School

Nanny

I was sad when my nanny died

Wishing she was alive and well
All my family was sad, especially me
So sad that she is gone

Sorry she had to go
A tear ran down my face
Doing fun stuff with her made me happy

Why did she have to go?
Hoping she will come back
Everybody was sad
Nobody could eat

Mother was sad
Y did she have to go?

Never forget you
A family was sad
Nobody was happy
Never go away
Y did you have to go cos we were really sad?

Did you have to go?
I will never forget you
Everybody was sad
Doing stuff with her made me smile.

Ryan Smith (12)
Earlham High School

The Clock

Tick-tock goes the clock,
Ever ticking, never stopping,
Tick-tock goes the clock,
Every minute the hand goes round,
Tick-tock goes the clock,
Ever ticking till the end,
Tick-tock goes the clock,
Every hour the bell chimes,
Tick-tock goes the clock,
Every day, forever,
Tick-tock goes the clock,
The sands of time go,
Tick-tock goes the clock,
The time falling from it,
Tick-tock goes the clock,
Ever giving, never faltering,
Tick-tock goes the clock,
Perpetually ticking and tocking,
Tick-tock goes the clock.

Antony Hinchliffe (14)
Earlham High School

My Companion

With my love I wish so well,
For someone secret who I can tell,
Someone kind and sensitive too,
Someone with advice on what to do.
Someone to welcome me when I come home,
A comforting hug when I'm feeling alone,
A faithful companion, loving and true,
All this I've found in a friend like you!

Sara Campbell (13)
Earlham High School

Poem

The sound of the sea
Deep down the life of others
Fish, dolphins and sharks
Depend on the sea

The waves hit the sand
With a gentle splash
Spraying white water into
The faces of watchers

Salt from the waves
Sting my face as I
Stand in the light breeze
The water hitting my legs

Sea, sea send me to sleep
Keep the sound of peace
Stay gentle and safe
Sea, sea let me be.

Joanne Oliver (13)
Earlham High School

Memories From September 11th

Cries and screams like thunder,
Dying as they wonder,
Hearts as cold as tundra,
As the people scream.

Children's parents dying,
Screaming as they're crying.
Dust and debris flying,
To never live their dreams.

Memories will vanish,
Dust and debris banish.
These terrible deeds abolish,
To rebuild these lives extreme.

Christopher Sillis (13)
Earlham High School

My Mate, Sam

Sam is always there for me,
When I need to talk.
Sam will listen patiently,
Beside me as we walk.
Sam's steps will never falter,
Walking side by side.
Across the park and wasteland,
Paths narrow and wide.
Sometimes I need to shed a tear
And only Sam will understand,
How sad I feel when I cry
And touch him with my hand.
The warmness in his eyes,
He never says a word
And yet he always listens well
And all I say, he's heard.
Our special place is in the woods,
Upon a fallen log.
Sam - my very special friend,
A golden retriever dog!

Abbie Sayer (13)
Earlham High School

Romance

The English talk about the weather,
Americans talk about their money,
But then the French talk about love . . .

Romance is a big thing in life,
But when it goes wrong, it's like you've been attacked with a knife.
People think it's a bit overrated,
But they most probably have never dated.
Sometimes you mix up love with lust,
You've got to get those feelings right and that's a must!
Make sure your lover treats you right,
Or you'll end up in a fight!

Rachel Bull (14)
Earlham High School

My Dog, Buster

You're big, brave and beautiful,
Soft and cuddly too,
You cry when I have to leave for school
And miss me like I miss you!
You're always there when I get home,
Bright-eyed and bushy-tailed too,
It isn't any wonder why I love you true,
Sometimes we play in the garden
Or if we feel fit, go for a run.
Then again if we feel like it,
We just laze around in the sun.
You're not just my companion,
You're a friend, faithful and true,
When I'm alone and missing something
Buster, baby, it's you.

Kirsty Batterbee (11)
Earlham High School

Can You Guess What I Am?

Brown and tasty,
I know its name,
Square and round,
It's got great fame.
Light and dark,
Milky and white,
It's full of sugar,
With each and every bite!
Always tickling taste buds,
Especially yours and mine,
When you've had a taste of me,
You'll zoom from size six to nine!
So can you guess what I am?
Yes! that's right, the chocolate man!

Vicky Rose (14)
Earlham High School

Me!

I looked at him, he looked at me,
I smiled, he smiled,
I felt happy.

I picked up my train and so did he,
I thought my myself, *wow, a new friend to play with me*.

I sat on the floor and began to play,
A simple game of follow me.

I raised one arm to scratch my head,
Then shouted at him to stop copying me.

I then called my mum to tell him to stop,
'Stop him Mum, stop, stop, stop.'

My mum came upstairs and stood by the door
And said to me, 'Who are you talking to?'
I replied to say, 'My friend standing there, he's copying me.'

She explained that I was only three
And the person that was copying me
Was not my friend, but my reflection
Getting the better of me!

Stacey Neale (14)
Earlham High School

Flying Through The Sky

A mystical bird
Flying through the sky
With its red, white, bright wings
You wouldn't believe the way it sings
The sweet noises it yells out
The comforting songs make you want to cry and shout
What a lovely bird it is
It's one you would like to see.

Brett Johnstone (11)
Earlham High School

Poisoned Denial

Lately I've been feeling dead inside,
Malicious pains like my gut's dried up and died.
Swivelling tornados attacking the blood left in my head,
Which once a deeper blue turned thicker red.

This house is full of ears but I can't talk to anyone,
All happiness aborted, watch as life comes undone.
People see through me, see through my heart, actions and lies,
I know you're after me, hurling toothpicks towards my eyes.

Your words slash through me, where they once would be kind,
Something pure to burn away the darkness in my mind.
Your voice should be the sound of sirens to a house on fire,
Now I see that you are just a manipulative liar.

I'm scratching and itching bought on by spiders under my skin,
Diverse from you, I am contrite towards my unjust sin.
You used to make me float, like a forgotten soul reaching for the sky,
It didn't matter what you'd say, when I was with you I couldn't cry.

I think perhaps a violent storm passed through you recently,
Your personality died, you're not the right person for me.
I'll always remember you close to my heart driving me insane,
A thought so sharp to rip through me and bleed out all the pain.

Laura Ryves (14)
Earlham High School

Grandad

I looked at my photos, old and new,
Photos of my grandad when he was two.
It reminded me of the times we had,
But together we are both happy and glad.
I asked my mum where he was,
She replied, 'In Heaven, up above!'

Ashley Lee (12)
Earlham High School

The Love Of My Life

My poem is about the love of my life
He gives me plenty of pleasure
And a little strife

We go for long walks together each day
He likes to eat
And is always ready to play

His eyes are shiny and brown
Big and round
Silky like a ballgown

He has soft, black, curly hair
It is very nice
Cuddly like a big bear

He always wears a black fur coat
Soft like his hair
It is very smooth just like a stoat

Each night he snores very loud
It keeps me awake
He must be dreaming up in a cloud

He is always being very happy
And full of noise
He is very kind, not at all snappy

Every day he gives me a kiss
I love him dearly
When I'm out, it's him I miss

Oh how much I love my dog, Toby.

Alice Steggles (14)
Earlham High School

Lord Of The Looks

His bright blue eyes
They hypnotise
His gorgeous voice
Makes me rejoice
He has nice hair
But it isn't fair
He's in Lord of the Rings
And other things
He looks so gentle
It makes me all sentimental
He looks so good
His name is Elijah Wood.

Robyn Kindred (14)
Earlham High School

Cats

They lay,
They play,
They always fall asleep,
They miaow,
They purr,
Aren't they so sweet?
Mice and birds,
Should oft' beware,
In case a pussy cat is there.
In the grass
Or by the fire curled,
They act as if
They own the world.

Aiden Keay (12)
Earlham High School

My Dog

Here is a story I want to tell,
Of a little Jack Russell I knew so well.
She was brown and white with a patch on her head,
She slept in the kitchen in a little round bed.
She lived with her family in quite a big house,
She could catch the birds and even a mouse.
She loved to run and jump so high,
You almost thought she'd reach the sky.
The house she lived in was full of fun,
The children after would run.
Nigel, Emma and Scott are her friends,
They were beside her to the end.
How old was she? I think she was six,
All her life she was up to tricks.
A cute little dog loved by all,
She'd run to you, no need to call.
She liked a chair, she'd hide her head,
Under the cushion for better than bed.
Watch out where you sit, she might be there,
Maybe you should choose another chair.
She has gone, no need to cry,
I'm sure she's watching from the sky.
She had a good life, you must agree,
It was great to be part of a family.

Emma Mulley (14)
Earlham High School

School

When I get up in the morning
'You'll be late,' comes my mum's warning
When I'm walking to school
I follow all the rules
I don't have to come very far
I just have to watch out for the cars
Six lessons each day
But they soon fade away
In English I do best
My maths can be a test
I keep on top of my work
So I won't look like a berk
We have homework by the ton
And it isn't any fun
By the time I go to bed
I can't get numbers out of my head
I try my best at PE
Even though I've got a dodgy knee
This is what school is to me!

Shannon Stone (11)
Earlham High School

Ice

As I stepped on the ice,
I rolled like a dice
And watched my skates slice through the ice,
The pattern I left was rather nice.
If I were to shut my eyes it would feel as if I were flying,
Swishing, sliding, swirling, gliding,
Falling on the wet, cold ice,
I thought my day was especially nice.

Voletta Bennett (11)
Earlham High School

My Dream Of The Future

One dim night I went to the future,
It was the year 3000.
Strange things were about to occur;
Strangest things like gravity had eased,
Kids used teleportation,
School didn't exist, teachers were seized.
How weird is this world?

Children were driving at any age.
They liked robot animals.
People were to sleep in a sleep cage,
Food was delivered by talking hawks,
Folks had robotic hearts, *ahh*
Bang, into my room my mother walks -
It was all a dream.

Karelia E Baptiste (11)
Earlham High School

October Hallowe'en

October, October is the month
Where we have a scary time.
October, October is the time
To get scared and have a laugh.
October, October, it must be the 31st,
Hallowe'en.

Hallowe'en, Hallowe'en is the time
The witches fly and the zombies rise.
Hallowe'en, Hallowe'en is the night
You see children in their dress-up all around.
Hallowe'en, Hallowe'en is the night
Vampires fly and kill.
Hallowe'en, Hallowe'en is the time
You should hide from the ghosts.

David Bradley (11)
Earlham High School

Peace

War should be forgotten
It brings lots of harm and hate
War should be forgotten
If you still want food on your plate

Nuclear war is such a mistake
Think of all the trouble you'd make

The UN and Middle East
Should try to get along
They should try to accept
They have both done lots of wrong

Try to listen to hippies
Even if they sound dippy

Peace and love throughout the world
That brings this poem to an end
So remember, next time war is struck
The world might come to an end.

Matthew Wellbourne (11)
Earlham High School

My Mother

Mum, you are the one it's plain to see,
You devoted your life, but not only to me.
You had another and another,
Can't you see? You are the perfect mother,
When we had our problems and our tears,
You were always near to help us through the years.
You always worked so very hard for all of us,
Never moaning or making a fuss.
No other mum cares as much as you do,
That is why Mum, we think the world of you.

Rhys Maskell (13)
Earlham High School

My Poem

Winter is around the corner
The water is turning to ice
When the day is here
The sun does not shine so warm and nice
The sun has slipped away
Hidden in the stars
Waiting for its other chance to come and stay
Waiting until it can show its face
When the sun comes back
Things will be OK
You can go unpack all your summer things
You stowed away
But summer isn't back yet
Things are still so dull
But don't worry about a thing
We've still got the mall.

Charlotte Johnstone (13)
Earlham High School

A Whistle

I heard a whistle, just the one,
Then it all began,
The ball was kicked for a long time,
I began to read a sign.

No, wait, the other team have the ball,
Are we in for a fall?
The ball is on boots,
He shoots.

Is it in his soul?
What a goal!

Emma Ireland (13)
Earlham High School

Winter

Winter is here
I can feel it in the air
Almost time for celebrations

The leaves have fallen
To the ground
Where they turn crisp and brown

Snow is falling
From the sky
Covering the countryside in a white blanket

Children are playing
Throwing snowballs
And building snowmen

The night is cold
So wrap up warm
Because winter can
Get to your bones.

Kirk Smith (13)
Earlham High School

Weeping Willow

Weeping willow, wipe your tears running down
Why do you always weep and frown?
Is it because he left you a day?
Is it because he could not stay?
On your branches he would swing,
You loved the happiness it would bring.
He found shelter under your shade,
You thought the laugher would never fade.
Weeping willow stop your tears,
There is something to calm your fears.
You think death as your goodbye forever part
And now he'll always be in your heart.

Kayleigh Baker (13)
Earlham High School

The Winter's Here

The winter's here,
the leaves are falling.
The morning birds
no longer calling.

The sun has gone,
gone far away.
The sun will come
back in May.

October nights,
so cold and dark.
When walking through
the empty park.

Animals hibernating,
underground.
Silence is here
and all around.

People sleeping,
without a care.
Don't they realise
that winter's here?

Abie Wilson (13)
Earlham High School

A Poem

There was a lady from Leeds
Who swallowed a packet of seeds,
In less than an hour
Her face was in flower
And her hair was all covered in weeds!

Sophie Moppett (14)
Earlham High School

I Love Sports

The touch of a ball,
The wind in your hair,
The tumble and fall,
I love sports.

The release of aggression,
The love and the passion,
The escape from depression,
I love sports.

The will to always stay fit,
The need to always improve,
The reason never to quit,
I love sports.

The wind in your hair,
The delight of a goal,
The utter despair,
I love sports.

Lewis Treloar (14)
Earlham High School

The Man From Spain

There was a young man from Spain,
Who looked like a weathervane,
His hair was messy and tame,
His walk was funny and lame,
He fell in love with a dame
Who bought him a brand new game,
He had to work for a dime,
To buy her some lovely lime,
So she had enough time
To make him some wine
And they both lived together so fine.

Zara Doy (13)
Earlham High School

Little Kitty

Little kitty
Small but strong
Has claws
Sharp and long

On your lap
Purring slightly
His body
Small and tiny

Stroking him
Swiftly but softly
Opens one eye
And lashes at me promptly

Little kitty
Small but strong
His claws
Sharp and long.

Lucy Payne (12)
Earlham High School

War!

Children crying and getting hurt
Guns firing and people dying
Houses being raided and destroyed
No food or drink, just bomb planes flying
Innocent people being killed
Mothers and fathers slaughtered in front of children's eyes
They hear a bomb, they run and hide
And that's it, the end of their suffering
It does not matter if you're black or white.

Georgina Marshall (14)
Earlham High School

My Sweet Tooth

Chocolate sundae, Walnut Whip,
Crunchie sticks and chocolate dip,
Suck a mint,
Chew a sweet, all the things I like to eat.
Hot chocolate with marshmallows afloat,
Also sweets with a sugar coat,
Cakes with icing,
Cakes which don't.
Oh and a can of Coke,
My sweet tooth must be crazy,
I'm gonna get fat and lazy,
Surely I am gonna hurt,
After I've had a chocolate Twirl.

Michaela Reeve (13)
Earlham High School

Autumn Leaves

I am a leaf,
Who's fallen from a tree,
About to be swept away.

What will happen to me when I'm swept away?
What will the children do when they want to play?

Adults taking away children's fun,
Is like taking away the golden sun.

I will be gone,
But not for long,
Autumn will come again.

James Drake (13)
Earlham High School

Untitled

Deep in the forest,
A secret lies,
Where no one ventures
And creatures hide.

No sunlight reaches
The forest floor
And ghostly whispers
Chill to the core.

Once such a magical place,
Colours of amber, gold and green,
Where animals roamed freely,
Now never to be seen.

A paradise, lost forever,
Just a memory left behind,
Destroyed by greed and power,
Demons of the human kind.

Hollie Reynolds (15)
Earlham High School

The Puma

It moves like shadows in the night,
It strikes like a snake.
Its claws are sharp as blades,
It is as strong as the ox.

In the trees its appearance is as thin as a phantom,
Its eyes glow like stars in the moonlight,
Its coat is as luxurious as a hotel suite.

Its fangs await the taste of blood,
Its movements are as silent as a mouse,
As its prey draws near, only luck can save it,
As it moves in for the kill.

John Gaughran (13)
Earlham High School

Holidays

When I go on holiday
And leave my gracious home,
How long will I have to stay
In the land where locals roam?

Will I decide to go abroad
Or will I stay in England?
Shall I go where the planes soared
Or shall I go on the sand?

Wherever I decide to go,
I'm sure it will be fun
And I hope that time will go slow,
So I can have more time in the sun.

Steven Guy (12)
Earlham High School

The Evilness Of Love

Love is painful, evil and wrong,
The pain emitted stays all life long.

Valentine's Day can't be right,
It's just wine and roses by candlelight.

Why do we waste our lives with love
And that so-called Cupid who comes from above?

So I ask you this as I come to an end,
Are you going to follow the trend

Of having love in your life
And marrying either man or wife?

Liam Hackett (13)
Earlham High School

Poem

This poem has no name
No lyrics, words or rhyme
Will get you no fame
Won't even be in time
Take a million years to write it
And still not be finished
Because
This poem has no name
No lyrics, words or rhyme
Will get you no fame
Won't even be in time
Take a million years to write it
And still not be finished
Because
This poem has no name
No lyrics, words or rhyme
Will get you no fame
Won't even be in time
Take a million years to write it
And still not be finished
Because . . .

Christina Nisbet (13)
Earlham High School

Autumn

Autumn days are round the corner,
With fresh brown leaves falling off the golden trees,
Jack Frost giving us all a chill throughout the day,
Round conkers bouncing up and down,
Darker nights are what we need
To see the flashing lights on one night indeed.

Leanne Stubbings (13)
Earlham High School

The Dark Alley

There's a dark alley,
No one dares to go there.

Death lurks there,
Robbery lurks there,
Betrayal lurks there.

There's a dark alley,
No one dares to go there.

Not even the bullies dare
Go into the dark alley,
Not even I dare to go
Into the dark alley.

There's a dark alley,
No one dares to go there.

Lee Hansell (13)
Earlham High School

Chocolate

C hocolate is so creamy and nice.
H ot chocolate just before bed.
O range chocolate tastes like oranges.
C aramel chocolate fills my tummy.
O nly one more piece to eat.
L ovely milky Cadbury chocolate.
A nimal chocolate biscuits are so scrumptious.
T erry's chocolates are so yummy.
E xtra large Easter eggs will fill my tummy.

Stacey Hawkins (13)
Earlham High School

Chocolate Cake

I love chocolate cake,
It's what I love to eat,
When I get it on my plate,
It really is a treat!

I love chocolate cake,
It's truly really sweet,
I really, really love its taste,
It surely can't be beat.

I love chocolate cake,
It's the best to me,
If I was allowed, I'd have it for
My breakfast, lunch and tea.

Ben Affleck (12)
Earlham High School

To Dad

Why did you leave me
When I was born?
Did you not think
Of the harm, my heart is torn.

As I grew up,
I thought of you always,
But my thoughts turned sour,
So sad were my days.

You have tried to get back
Into my life,
To buy my love with your gifts,
But no money can replace
The time you have missed.

Stevie Green (13)
Earlham High School

Sweet Things

Not a girl, but sweets?
Hot cherry lips,
Liquorice whips,
Toblerone standing like a pyramid
And all the jelly babies hid,
Toasted mushrooms standing like soldiers,
Rolling Chewits just like boulders,
Old men's candy canes.

Shimmering sherbet in the rain,
Bountys bouncing as if they were on a bouncy castle,
Minstrels being rascals,
Candyfloss just like clouds,
All sweets in a big crowd,
Jelly beans more sweeter than baked beans,
Kinder Eggs being seen,
White on the outside, toy in-between.

Chubba Hubba glazed like marbles,
Gum always making marvels,
Slabs of toffee, hard and knobbly,
Aeros ever so wobbly,
Aniseed balls, just like cannonballs
Mars far, far away.

Cream eggs, yellow and white,
If you think they're delicious, come and have a bite,
Rainbow dust, colours so bright,
Turkish Delight dusted in white,
Polos always perfect but are they really worth it?

Too much to choose from, not very cheap,
Maybe I'll settle for a girl,
But she's got to be sweet!

Thomas Mills (12)
Earlham High School

My Haikus On Computers

Extremely useful
annoying when they crash down
find information

equipment needed
printers, speakers, scanners, disks
can be expensive

helps you with homework
download music and play games
send e-mails to friends

faster with broadband
technologically advanced
excellent value!

Rachael Goulding (13)
Earlham High School

Angry

My face is bright red
I'm slamming the door
They can hear me next door
I'm as red as a cherry
I can't take it anymore

Doors slamming
Feet stomping
Hair pulling
Eyes popping
Mind blowing
I'm a volcano about to blow my top.

Kelly Plummer (11)
Earlham High School

A Nature Poem

The fields are green
The cows look mean
The rabbits are keen
The squirrels have been

The buttercups are yellow
The clouds look like pillows
The trees are like willows
The howl of the wind bellows

The farmers whistle
Pricks are sharp on a thistle

The roads are quiet
The tractors' engines quit

The only sound
Are birds talking to each other.

Gemma Green (14)
Earlham High School

Mysterious Eyes!

I opened the door
and what did I see?
Two big eyes staring at me,
Big and bold,
The air became cold,
Then I screamed,
My mum came down
And said, 'What's wrong?'
I said, 'I saw something in the room!'
My mum went through
To see what it was,
But in the end
It was only my dog.

Stacey Mann (13)
Earlham High School

Footy

Football is the best,
It's better than the rest.
Football it's a joy,
To beat the boys.
The fans go wild,
The footballers are tired.
Football is the best,
It's better than the rest.

Dean Kalantson (15)
Earlham High School

Hell Broth

Round about the cauldron go,
Into it these things must go,
Black and hairy spider legs,
Slimy slugs and frogs' legs,
Children's orange carrot stick,
Mush it up to make it thick,
With blood, bones and dirty stones,
You must eat this to be fit.

Chelsea Walker (12)
Earlham High School

What's For Afters?

Sponges filled with buttercream
Banoffee pie is a dream
Then there is Angel Delight
What shall I have for afters tonight?
All these things sound nice to me
But I think I'll have a bowl of ice cream.

Kelly Forbes (12)
Earlham High School

His True Love At First Sight!

This is true love,
like two flying doves making love, above.

I hear my heart beating fast,
I think this love will always last.

I see her eyes shining bright,
that's how I saw her at first sight.

Her voice is like a bluebird singing,
she's not like any other human being.

I love her, I love her.

She's like a perfect rose,
beautiful and fine . . .

That's why I want her to be all mine.

Harriette Simmons (14)
Earlham High School

Who Am I?

My eyes are the stars,
Glistening in the night's sky.

My hair is the lush green grass,
As birds flutter by.

My fingertips are the touch of pearls.

My smile is the sun,
Lightening up the world.

Who am I?

Laura Watkinson (14)
Hethersett High School

Megan

Megan
Megan
Poor
Petrified
Pregnant
And treated like an outcast

Megan
Sixteen years old . . .
Well, almost
Getting bigger
But not out of choice
Too young to be responsible

Some seem to cope well
But not me
Straggly hair
And stuck living in
A damp, cramped flat
With Mum and sister
In the seedy suburb of London

Megan.

Laura Brewis (12)
Hethersett High School

September 11th 2001

In New York City
The winds will blow
Between the Twin Towers
Which stood days ago
Mark our place where
The rubble lies
Which is now safe
From the terrible skies
We are the dead
Who lived days ago
Our graves are now
Marked down below
Loved and were loved
And now we lie
In the rubble of
New York City.

The plane went whooshing
And weeping through the sky
Everyone looked at it
Swirled up high
But nobody knew they
Were going to die.

The plane went *crash*
Bang, crash
All I remember is
A big bright flash
Now I know exactly
What that was
The Twin Towers
Were on fire, on fire, on fire
They came crumbling and
Crashing to the ground
Where the loved ones were to be found.

We pray this very day, 2 years onward
That attacks like this
Will never, never happen again.

Laura Wiltshire (13)
Hethersett High School

I Is For Identity

I is not you, I is myself,
I is plainly, simply me,
I is no one else at all,
I is for identity.

I is working, every part,
I is hearing, I can see,
I is not different in that way,
I is for identity.

I is individual,
I is no one else, just me,
I is also part of a crowd,
I is for identity.

I is black or I is white,
I is what I want to be,
I is happy as I am,
I is for identity.

Amber Curtis (13)
Hethersett High School

Untitled

So I have a new name - student,
Strange that my name should take away from me,
Who I am, my identity, my individuality,
Make me part of a crowd,
To be treated the same as everybody else,
To be one face among many,
One person among hundreds,
Living life unknown except for results and grades,
This is having the name, student.

Lewis Cletheroe (13)
Hethersett High School

What Do You See?

I looked in the mirror,
What did I see?
Not black, not white,
But me, only me.

Pale peach face,
Sea-blue eyes,
Snowy-white teeth,
That's little old me.

Yes, I looked in the mirror,
What did I see?
Not fat or thin,
But me, only me.

Little elf ears,
Rose-red lips,
Golden-sand hair,
Yes! That's me.

Oh I looked in the mirror,
What did I see?
A teenage girl,
Smiling back at me.

That must be me.

If you look
In the mirror,
What do you see?

You may see black,
You may see white,
But you won't see me,
No, you won't see me.

Marie Ellis (14)
Hethersett High School

What Do I See?

I've just been born, what do I see?
My mummy and daddy looking at me,
Dribbling and crying, drinking my milk,
My head is so soft, like the feel of silk.
I've just turned one, what do I do?
I start making noises like a cow going *moo, moo.*
I'm two years old now, ready to walk,
I've even learnt now how to pick up my fork.
My brother is now born, as sweet as a stick of rock,
As he listens to his baby clock going *tick-tock.*
At five years of age, I'm now well into school,
Learning and reading, I think I'm really cool.
I started middle school when I was eight,
I walked to school, never was late.
Double figures now, yes I'm ten,
My writing is much neater now, I have a fountain pen.
Now such a big girl at the high school,
Now all my friends think I'm really cool.
I catch the bus at the top of my road,
My bags are so full, such a heavy load.
Yes! Now I'm a teen, confident, and keen,
Finding a job and dancing all the time,
Just take a look at me and you will see that I . . .
Shine!

Alannah Short (13)
Hethersett High School

My Identity Poem!

I looked in the mirror,
what did I see?
Not black, not white,
but me, just me.

A smooth, round face,
with green, sparkling eyes,
with clean white teeth
like sweet white lies.

I looked in the mirror,
what did I see?
A small young girl,
who's precious to me.

A long, pointed nose
and rosy-red lips.
With long, curly hair
that shines to the tips.

I looked in the mirror,
what did I see?
A big, happy smile,
gazing back at me.

I'm not black,
not white,
not Asian,
not even Indian,
just little old me,
that's what I see!

Gemma Needham (13)
Hethersett High School

The Animals Inside Me . . .

There is a cat in me,
Sneaky and suspicious,
Slyer than a fox
And sometimes mischievous,
As quiet as a mouse,
Whilst hunting its prey,
But can be fierce and fiery,
Throughout the day,
Hiding round corners,
To be alone and free,
Never giving in,
That easily
Sometimes moody, playful and fun,
Many happy times
Spent out in the sun!

The monkey in me
Can be very cheeky,
Running and jumping and playing around,
But has been known to try hard
And have fun in the yard,
But is sometimes so quiet,
You cannot hear a sound,
A joker and a friendly mate,
Always happy and mucking around.

There is a tortoise in me,
Trying hard to be free,
My favourite animal,
Trying to escape from me,
Thinking things over,
While searching for clover
And taking things slowly,
As they come,
Lounging around,
Without worrying at all
And sometimes can't be bothered
To do much at all!

There is a butterfly in me,
Aiming to fly high,
Spreading its wings
Soaring into the sky,
Gracefully landing,
In a colourful world,
Exploring surroundings,
Whilst wings are uncurled,
Aiming to fly higher,
Than ever before,
Believing and hoping,
She will open the new door,
Clever and thoughtful,
Laid back and relaxed,
An imaginative world open,
Not tightly locked and latched.

There is a lion in me,
Angry and mad,
Roaring and fighting,
Upset and sad,
Answering back,
Jumping into a rage,
I try to keep this lion,
Locked in its cage!

These animals are what make me special and complete,
Without them I would suffer and admit to defeat,
They always help me along, each day by day
And help me find a better tomorrow, today,
They came into the sunshine of my world
And made a difference to my life,
Without them, I would not survive
At all . . .

Emma Dudzinski (13)
Hethersett High School

What Did I See?

I looked in the mirror,
What did I see?
Black or white?
It was me!

With long blonde hair
And deep blue eyes,
Rosy-red lips
And horrible thighs.

Elegant legs
And beautiful arms,
People turn their heads,
Got all boys in charms.

This girl I saw,
Was looking at me,
I thought to myself,
What does she see?

She saw me,
Just me!
The girl in the mirror,
Her name was Vicki.

I looked in the mirror,
What did I see?
Black or white?
It was me!

Vicki MacKenzie (13)
Hethersett High School

The Keeper!

There is a cat in me . . . sharp paws ready to strike . . .
I might seem gentle but there is a different side to me

There is a squirrel in me . . . you could see me
at one moment and the next I'd be hiding away . . .
if you look for me you wouldn't find me
'cause I am the keeper of the squirrel

There is a butterfly in me . . . floating in mid-air
just chilling out . . . I am the keeper of the butterfly

There is a lion in me . . . with a golden coat of fur . . .
sensing things in the air . . . ready to attack
the lion in me is usually locked up in a cage
but sometimes I leave the cage undone
I am the keeper of the lion

All these animals are me
they belong inside me
they stay inside me
I am the keeper of the zoo!

Kelly Rogers (13)
Hethersett High School

Wilderness

There is a parrot in me . . . loud and bright . . .
able to escape and fly wherever it pleases . . .
colourful and chatty . . . sometimes cheeky . . .
I will always have this parrot.

There is a snake in me . . . with a sharp, forked tongue . . .
painful bites . . . I'm not proud of this snake
but I will always have it.

There is a tiger inside me . . . razor-sharp claws . . .
ready to pounce . . . this is my anger . . .
unleashing itself on an unlucky victim . . .
I will always have this tiger.

There is a little elephant in me . . . lost without its herd . . .
wary of strangers but playful with friends . . .
strong yet emotional . . .
I will always have this little elephant.

I own this zoo, but I don't hold the key . . .
the animals come and go as they please . . .
these animals make me who I am . . .
they are me . . . they always will be part of me . . .
I love and hate these animals . . .
they are my wilderness.

Rachel Willis (13)
Hethersett High School

The Animals In Me

The fox in me likes to stay anonymous
Picking on the weak
Picked on by the strong
Villain of the night

The bird in me is ambitious
Swooping, soaring higher than the sun
It wishes to be free forever
Cooped up, it can do nothing

The monkey in me is cheeky and chirpy
Gliding, jumping, hopping from one place to another
An entertainer, a fun lover
Joker of the animal pack

The snake in me is dangerous
Hissing and swaying, it waits innocently, unnoticed
It takes one thing to set it off
Then it springs into venomous action

These are my animals
These animals are me
Often they are kept away
But sometimes they are free.

Stephen Sanders (13)
Hethersett High School

Wilderness

There is a bird in me . . .
wings to fly me wherever I want,
whenever I want . . .

There is a mouse in me . . .
quiet, shy and when I'm scared,
I hide away . . .

There is an eagle in me . . .
daring to go where others don't . . .

There is a dolphin in me . . .
friendly and tame . . .

There is a snake in me . . .
slithery, slippery and with
many dark secrets . . .

These are the animals in me . . .

They set me free,
they tease me,
they help me be me
and they make me stronger.

Chloe Cabutto (13)
Hethersett High School

Wilderness

I am a squirrel inside
I am small, fast and furry
I am soft and sweet
But I can be angry and fight back
I can go where I like
Hide everywhere
Be anywhere!

I am a duck inside
I am scared of putting my toes
In the cold water
I am feathery and I stand out
I love following my family
Along the riverside

I am a monkey inside
I am a cheeky chimp
I swing from tree to tree
Free as can be
I play around with my friends
But I like spending time
With my family

I am a kingfisher inside
I am bright and colourful
I fly high above the treetops
I sit on the tree branches
I have a loud voice
Which I use well

I am a cage and a key
I cage things in and I set good things free
I have to keep bad things in
Although sometimes they creep out
I let out all of my good things
Except some hide within
I try my hardest to control everything
But sometimes I fail.

Danielle Mills (13)
Hethersett High School

Wilderness

There is a butterfly in me . . .
It's colourful and bright,
Flittering around in the morning sunshine.
Wings flapping rapidly like flashes of light,
Flying high and low.

There is a dolphin in me . . .
Jumping in and out of the cool,
Turquoise sea, swimming quickly,
Eagerly waiting to see and meet new people.

There is a lion in me . . .
Lying in the long, sharp green grass
Waiting to pounce and roar loudly
At the sight of something horrible.

There is a kangaroo in me . . .
Jumping around, always looking for things
To do or see, going somewhere new,
Experiencing new hobbies.

Lucy Placzek (13)
Hethersett High School

Different Faces, Different Races

Everyone should be able to walk down the street
Without fear of the people they're going to meet
It doesn't matter if you're black, pink or white
The colour of your skin shouldn't start a fight

You mustn't let them taunt you just by the colour of your skin
You should hold your head high and say you are going to win
You mustn't let the abuse ruin your life
Yet you shouldn't resort to a gun or a knife.

Jennie Bradley (12)
Hethersett High School

Me!

I looked in the mirror
What did I see?
A girl with glasses
And as lively as can be

With brown eyes
Loves to dance
And listening to music
And as pretty as can be

Who is twelve years old
With brown hair
Loves having fun
And takes a lot of care
Which has to be said

When you look
In the mirror
What do you see?
It has to be
Me!

Leanne Bolingbroke (12)
Hethersett High School

Methias, The Shadow

Eyes of a hawk,
Ears of a hare,
Cunning as a fox,
Strong as a bear.

As swift as a shadow,
As silent as the dead,
He's part of the night
With his cloak dark as lead.

Methias is his name,
The master thief is here,
So lock away your treasures,
For they're sure to disappear.

A watchman's looking out,
Standing with his hound,
Not a scent in the air,
Not a stir nor a sound.

No *whoosh* of his cloak,
No clomping of boots,
Just a glimpse of his shadow,
As he adds to his loot.

Then he blends with the darkness
And slinks into the gutter,
His bag brims with his hoard,
As the guard begins to mutter.

Many will try to catch him
And all who do, shall fail,
As Methias, the shadow,
Will never leave a trail.

Jamie Wiggins (13)
Hethersett High School

My Little Sister

I wanted a baby sister
more than anything in the world.

Whenever I pulled a wishbone,
I wished for a baby girl.

On the day the baby arrived,
my dad rang to tell,
I had a baby sister
and she was fit and well.
We decided to name her Fiona.

She smells like a rose,
from the top of her dark-haired head
to the bottom of her little baby toes.

She's warm and soft
and pink and round.
She is the prettiest baby
that was ever found.

She feeds like a piglet
and sounds like one too.

She's always hungry,
both day and night.
To keep her happy
is quite a fight.

She is a full time job
for an army of ten
or twenty if the army is made up of men.

I love my baby sister
and I am glad I have found a lifetime companion
and a lifetime best friend.

Rachel Hill (12)
Hethersett High School

A Dream, Or Reality?

'I have a dream
That one day, this nation
Will rise up and live the true meaning of its creed:
That all men are created
Equally'.

I have a dream too
That someday there will
Be a world without war,
People will link hands in the
Circle of friendship.

Is there a person, creature or being
Who'll help us?
An angel who'll lay their silken hand
On this cut, bleeding world.

Father, Father help us,
Send the white dove to rest upon us all.

We are bacteria, creating a pandemic of
Illness, despair and death.

Yet there are those willing to pay the price of their lives,
To make a difference to mankind.
Martin Luther King was one.

Are you?

Hannah Davis (12)
Hethersett High School

Myself

The name's Nick,
Nick Payne.
Relaxed yet always tense,
A stranger and a friend.
Open but secure,
I break, then I mend.

The name's Nick,
Small and strong,
Blue-eyed,
Dark, spiky hair.
Never *too* tidy,
Skin quite fair.

The name's Nick,
Nick Payne
And proud of it.
The name's Nick,
The name's Nick.

Nick Payne (12)
Hethersett High School

The Identity Snatcher

The identity snatcher is big and tall
And stands outside the lunchtime hall,
Or sometimes even at the loos,
With his messy hair and his big black shoes,
Some of the kids he kicks and curses
And forces them to hand over their purses,
These kids were once happy and smart,
But now the snatcher's taken them apart,
They were kids who used to have many goals,
Until he took away their souls,
Now these kids live in fear,
Because they know the identity snatcher is near.

Corrie Moxon (12)
Hethersett High School

Feelings In Life

You can lose yourself
Inside my mind
There's so many things going on
So many feelings that I can't describe

Take a look deeper
Through the tangles of my mind
See my personality
The person that's behind

See how I'm usually happy
See how I make people laugh
See all the friends that I have in this world
See the deeper things in life

See through to my true colours
See through me
See through to the person behind
Gaze deep into my mind

All of the mysteries
That go on in my life
See all of the people crying
See all of the strife

See through to my harder side
How I don't cry
See to the strong personality
That I cannot hide

This is me
This is my life
A part of me's in this poem
This is my life.

Claire Ashby (12)
Hethersett High School

I For Identity

I am I, but why am I?
What shall I do or see?
And how could I, if I should try,
Become a better me?

I look up to the stars in the dark night sky
And they wisely wink at me,
Saying, 'You need to look for the greater good,
Your true identity.'

I'd like to help others and I'd like to learn
To get them to follow me
And to grow the good inside them too,
So happy we could be.

To help each other every day
And give your best for free,
To friends and family, those in need,
How can anyone disagree –

That neither you nor I exist alone
And I would rather be
Us, instead of me, myself,
A worldwide family.

Benjamin Wright (12)
Hethersett High School

Will

Will,
Will,
Poor old Will,
Whacked with that stick,
That will never do.

For the mistake of a foe,
He did not know,
He took the pain,
But there was no gain.

He went to knight school,
Hoping for a duel,
With no armour to wear,
He did not dare.

Will,
Will,
Poor old Will.

Thomas Alden (12)
Hethersett High School

Dream

I lay in my field filled with paper flowers,
I relax in the grass and dream for hours.
Candyfloss clouds slowly drifting by,
The hazelnut sunshine in the early morning sky.

Wild flower scent of pear drops and rose,
Autumnal colours, toffee apples and cloves.
Bonfires crackle to see out the year,
Remembering friends and family so dear.

Lemon bonbon daffodils stand in a row,
Sparkling cherryade from waterfalls flow.
I can drink and eat all night with my friends,
But when the alarm clock shouts, that's where the dream ends.

Andrea Leggett (12)
Hethersett High School

Bob Burnquist, My Favourite Skater

The horrific anger in his face when his board snaps into pieces
and the adrenaline he needs to clear the loop.
As he places his board onto the lip, a slight tingle rushes through his body and then when he drops in, his blood rushes to his head as fast as a cheetah!

When he's about to do the loop with the roof gap off,
his legs feel like jelly and as he drops in, he swirls from side to side
and goes up the loop, clears the gap
and falls absolutely unpleasantly.

The joyful dreams he must have when he goes to bed,
thinking of all the kids he has encouraged
to skate for fun and not for life!

Tom Milne (12)
Hethersett High School

The Hindu's Poem

Born on Sunday
In the city of Delhi

Lived on Monday
Flying my kite

Died on Tuesday
Burning on a pyre

Reborn on Wednesday
Flew as a bird

Lived on Thursday
As a bird of prey

Died on Friday
Shot by bird hunters

Reborn on Saturday
Into Moksha.

Philip Morgan (12)
Hethersett High School

Potter

Potter, Potter,
The boy who stayed alive,
With Voldemort on his tail, how does he survive?
He goes to Hogwarts, the wizardry school
And all of his friends think he is so cool.
Harry stays with his uncle after summer term,
He wants to go to Hogwarts so he can learn.
Harry has shaggy hair and a lightning scar.
In Year 2 he drove a flying car,
His parents are dead,
Harry has a photo by his bed.
He loves to play Quidditch, it is his game,
Gryffindor Seeker is his name.
Potter has Hedwig, the snowy owl,
Vernon will moan if he hears it howl.
He lives at number 4 Privet Drive,
Voldemort doesn't want him to live.
Hagrid is his mate,
A giant who is great.
Ron has ginger hair,
He always has to swear.
Hermione is so smart,
She plays such a big part
In the life of
Potter, Potter!

Samantha Bingham (12)
Hethersett High School

Teenage Life!

I looked in the mirror and what did I see?
A spotty old teenager staring back at me,
With spots on his face and hair on his chest,
Oh why at this age do we never look our best?

You wake every morning with one more spot,
You try to get rid of it with all the cream you've got,
Your girlfriend's all moody, it's getting you down,
All you want to do is howl like a hound

And when you get home, you have a pile of homework
That needs to be done
And why can't you go back to when you were young?
When you're not in school,
You're down the skatepark trying to be cool.

It wasn't all that bad in the end,
You've got your looks back and you've got a girlfriend,
You've been through the worst and your life is ahead,
You're not at school, you're at work instead.

But one day your children will go through it too,
So you have to remember how it was for you.
It is amazing how the time does fly,
Before you know it you will be saying goodbye.

Daniel Orford (12)
Hethersett High School

Daisy

Daisy
I love the way her eyes twinkle,
When the sun shines brightly.

I love the way she smiles,
It lights up my day (completely).

I love it when I go round and she's watching Ceebeebies
Because it makes me so happy
When she's laughing at the Tweenies!

I love the way she looks at me,
Because she looks so sweet and innocent!

But when the day is coming to an end,
She's so tired and sleepy.

I love the way she lays there,
So snuggled and huggled.

Now I know why she gets away with so much more!

That's Daisy,
So sweet and innocent!

Ashley Clayton (13)
Hethersett High School

I Met A Boy At School

I met a boy at school,
He's very, very cool.
Brown hair, brown eyes
And not very organised.

He's not quite tall,
But not very small.
He likes football
And rubbish at the rules.

He's got lots of friends,
But that's not the end.
I live round the bend
Of his other friend.

He always eats his tea
And plays out with me.
He gets grounded
Every other week.

Jade Dodds (12)
Hethersett High School

What Am I?

I can dive down to Earth like a preying hawk,
The wind teasing me on.
No living thing can resist my touch.
I am nature's mirror, reflecting the sky
And at night, the stars.

I gather silently, my destiny unknown.
I tear over jagged rocky pinnacles and peaks,
Grinding like a millstone as I pass,
Ever hiding from my enemy in the sky.

I am water and my gift is life.

Oliver Bayfield (12)
Hethersett High School

Look At Me

Look at me in my wheel
Some think I'm happy
But this is who I feel

People stare at me every day
I get no privacy
I tell them all to go away
And stop looking at me

I know they feed me every day
I know he is my friend
But they will not take a hint
I'm coming to an end

I'm a hamster, small and cute
But please leave me alone
I think I'm going to shoot
And make my small name known.

Jonathan Ball (12)
Hethersett High School

My Love Is Like . . .

My love is like a double-decker bus
That goes and goes 'til it's far enough,
My love is like a big ferry boat
That goes along an ever-going moat.

My love is like a shrivelled green pea,
Not big enough for the world to see,
It's also like a rusty brown nail
That's trapped in a door like it is frail.

My love is like the Heaven and Earth,
It's good and bad like Heaven and birth.

Naomi Larner (12)
Hethersett High School

'I' Is For Identity

You look at me and see a girl,
Who seems as if she has no care in the world,
Nobody can get her down and upset her,
Nobody can make her cry and feel pressured.

You see a girl who's confident,
Holds her head high and never backs away,
Nobody knows that really she's scared and worried,
Nobody knows how much she hates every day.

You see a girl who tries her hardest,
Someone that would never give up on a dream,
Nobody can tell that really she's always dreaming,
Nobody can see that her dreams are better than reality.

You see a girl who's surrounded by popularity,
She's funny and never backs down,
Nobody cares that this girl isn't real,
Nobody cares about how this fake girl must feel.

You see a girl who's happy,
Someone who never seems to cry,
Nobody sees that really she's unhappy,
Nobody sees how much pain is killing her inside.

I look at me and see a girl,
A fake who's scared to show the real her,
Who made herself from the best of everyone
And won't let her true self be known.

Never try to be someone you're not,
Don't hide yourself beneath a fake,
People should like you for the real you,
I've learnt that 'cause I made this mistake.

Natalie Lister (13)
Hethersett High School

World's Best Mum

Her heart was lost the day she met
The man who changed her world.
The story starts, the tale unfolds,
As here it will be told.

The love she has is all divine,
It wraps her family well,
She guards and watches over all
And so all danger quells.

She dresses a crab in no time at all,
Whilst answering your call.
Her cooking never ceases to amaze,
The countless mouths she saves.

Rely on her to plan your week,
To organise events,
To shuffle programmes,
E-mail friends and never ever be late.

Her week is full, is full of us,
Brownies, church and fêtes,
Of badminton, horses, going out
And cooking for our mates.

Overall I want to say,
She is a friend to me
And I want to be like her one day,
For all the world to see.

Laura Webster (12)
Hethersett High School

I Is For Identity

I am defined by my fingertips,
My eyes give me away,
The colour of my hair, be it blonde, black or grey,
This is who I am and this who I'll be.

My voice belongs to me, not anybody else,
The colour of my skin encasing me inside,
The shape of my body, which I cannot hide,
This is who I am and this is who I'll be.

My body DNA distinguishes me from others,
The bite of my teeth leaves a print of my jaw,
There's been nothing else like this before,
This is who I am and this is who I'll be.

You have an identity much like myself,
Nothing can defeat you at being yourself,
This is who you are and this is who you'll be,
So never ever doubt your identity.

Suzanne Chamberlin (12)
Hethersett High School

Reflection

I look in the mirror, what do I see?
A reflection of a soft, round face,
Big bright blue sparkling eyes,
Rosy-red cheeks,
A smile beaming from one ear to the other,
Long, sleek, dark blonde, shiny hair,
A face full of happiness, love, laughter,
Hey, I know that face, it's me . . .
Maria.

Maria Scott (12)
Hethersett High School

No Love?

(Inspired By Black Eyed Peas)

I looked in the mirror
What did I see?
Neither love nor peace
Only hatred and terror

Children dying
After battles and wars
Parents crying
Like there are no more laws

People on the ground
Whose families they've lost
None neither seen nor found
Because they've had to pay a cost

Where is the love?
Where is the love?
They need help from someone
But no one is helping them up from above

Hopefully someday
There will be peace
Where there is no more war
And when the love will *increase.*

Lauren Benka (12)
Hethersett High School

Shallow

Why are you so shallow? Please tell me,
You look at my outside but not inside me.
Don't look at my spots, don't look at my hair,
Don't speak behind my back and constantly stare.

Why? is the question, why can't we be a team?
You're always picking on me, you're always so mean!
I know I don't wear make-up, I know I am not pretty,
But inside I am beautiful,
Come on, you're so picky!

My feelings are important and so are yours too,
But if you see I care about you, so you should care for me too,
You compare me to famous models,
Oh please, give me a break!
Even if I did wear make-up, I wouldn't look like Naomi Campbell!

This is the end, this has to stop,
This is the end of your nasty plot . . .
I am drained and angry, I can't take anymore!
It has also become an almighty bore!
I am what I am
And you have made me more independent and strong!
And I will fight you for evermore!

Emma Lester (12)
Hethersett High School

My False Identity

I'm sitting here, thinking about it,
How people see me, think of me
And I realise, I just don't fit in,
Just not what they want me to be.

These insecurities I don't reveal,
These thoughts I try to hide;
This person I try not to be,
This person, deep inside.

I thought they liked me, I really did
And liked me for who I am
And I realise, I just don't fit in
And I don't think I ever can.

The dismal grey, the surrounding mist,
Now everything is wrong.
No one really understands,
They all think I've moved on.

My identity is a false one,
They'll never know the true me
And I realise, I just don't fit in,
I'm not what they want to see.

Hannah Frost (12)
Hethersett High School

Racism

What would the world be like
Without the hatred of black?
I just want to say to all the racists out there,
I'm not gonna take that!

Who are we to judge
By the colour of skin?
Stopping it doesn't have to be a dream,
It could really happen!

The black are just like us,
Apart from coloured skin,
So shut up and stop making a fuss,
Because you're not gonna win!

What would people think
If freedom wasn't allowed?
If you hate the black, I'm telling you,
This racism's got to stop, now!

Sarah Wyatt (12)
Hethersett High School

If I Could Take A Photo

If I could take a photo of everyone in the world,
What would I see through my camera?
Would I see men and women, boys and girls,
Tall people, short people,
People with curls,
White people, black people,
People in-between,
People with a freckled face
And people who don't like to be seen?
You can think of me whatever you want to think,
I don't really care,
But it's what's inside that counts,
Not race, looks or hair!

Graham Jermy (13)
Hethersett High School

Crippled

Life is not worth living,
when everyone does stare
and laugh and point and whisper,
cos you're in a wheelchair.

When you're feeling awkward,
you are now crippled for life,
it makes you have thoughts
of slitting wrists with knives.

People stand there goggling,
cos you are not the same,
you're suffering inside
from all the vocal pain.

The names fall like hammer blows,
falling to the head,
spaz, cripple, weirdo,
you wish you could be dead.

You are not much different
from people in the chairs,
so think what you would be like
and consider them in your prayers.

Laurence Martin (12)
Hethersett High School

Nightmare

I gaze up at the sparkling stars
The wish for once I dreamt about Mars
But every night I fall asleep
I wake up with a sudden beat

I lie afraid up in my bed
Thinking what my mother said
'Nothing in nightmares is ever real'
Even that gigantic wheel

I shiver and shake
But continue to bake
Up in my bed
The ache hurts my head

I finally feel I drift off to sleep
But all of a sudden *beep, beep, beep*
It was 7 o'clock
I heard a knock

I wonder who
Had big green shoes?
I could see under the bedroom door
The handle went down
My spine shivered

The man in my nightmare!
No, it couldn't be
But yes it was
Now I could see he had come for me!

Ryan Turner (12)
Hethersett High School

Who Are You?

You don't know my name,
I don't have one.
You don't know my age,
I don't have one.

You don't see my eyes,
I don't have any.
You don't see my ears,
I don't have any.

You don't hear my voice,
I don't have one.
You don't hear my breath,
I don't have one.

I sneak up on you like a cheetah on its prey,
When I take hold, I never let go.
Who, when and where am I?
I'm all around; I'm your worst fear.

You are *dead!*

Emma Griffiths (12)
Hethersett High School

I Is For Identity

I skulk around my midnight lair
All alone without a care
When suddenly some movement there
I go to check the corner bare
Don't worry, a false alarm

I run up to my owner's room
My face like a sensor, my tail like a broom
Around the outside door I loom
When swiftly a flicker in the gloom
Don't worry, a false alarm

The door it quickly opens wide
I attempt to run inside
I run for the cupboard then I will hide
But something's moving at my side
Don't worry, a false alarm

I have checked around the house
I stop to scratch, it's just a louse
I see a movement, I use my nose
It was a foe but just a mouse
Soon it's dead and that wasn't a false alarm.

Will Watts (12)
Hethersett High School

A White Man's Poem

I looked in the mirror
What did I see?
I saw a lonely old man
Looking back at me

With red, saggy eyes
All wriggly and old
Should I give up
Or die of the cold?

Remembering the days
When I was a young lad
When plenty of friends
And the fun we had

If you looked in the mirror
What would you see?
I saw a young man
Looking back at me.

Rachel Yeomans (12)
Hethersett High School

Untitled

S mart and
A greeable
R ealistic too
A rtistic and
H appy, just like you!

E nthusiastic and
D aring
W onderful too
A nd very
R eliable and
D ependant
S ame as you!

Sarah Edwards (13)
Hethersett High School

Who Am I?

I stand in the doorway,
like a shadowy silhouette,
just to remind you,
so you don't forget.

I am everywhere you look,
you have turned white as a sheet
and now the day is over,
you try to fall asleep.

But it really isn't working,
I will just keep on haunting,
you know what you have done,
just the thought of me is daunting.

My name is Guilt.

Danielle Carle (12)
Hethersett High School

Deep Down Inside

Deep down inside, you are a normal person,
Not the girl that stands in the corner alone,
Not the person crying by herself,
Nobody asks you to come round, on the phone.

Deep down inside, you are a pretty girl,
Not a spotty geek with big glasses,
Not a teacher's pet,
Everybody stares at you in classes.

Deep down inside, you are one groovy gal,
You just show people who you are,
You just show people what you can do,
Deep down inside, you are one shining star . . .

Sophie Harvey (12)
Hethersett High School

I Is For Identity

I am what I am
And I'll be what I be
It's not up to you
But it is up to me.

You never will find
Someone else just like me
You can search all you like
And then you will see.

That everyone's different
Like each and every bee
Just like a potato
Just like a green pea.

I don't care what I am
As wide as the sea
As quiet as a mouse
But I'm happy as can be.

I am what I am
And I'll be what I be
It's not up to you
But it is up to me.

Louise Brownsey (12)
Hethersett High School

The Wilderness

There's a chimpanzee in me . . . jumping to
trees . . . climbing up high nearly touching
the top . . . hanging around with my friends.

There's a beluga in me . . . as white as can be . . .
a lump as big as a ball on my head . . .
swimming gracefully . . . getting lonely when
my friends go away.

There's a dolphin in me . . . jumping out
of the ocean . . . racing against each other . . .
having lots of fun . . . making friends . . .
travelling far . . . seeing places.

There's an orca in me . . . swimming with
my large family . . . eating lots of fish . . .
rubbing against rocks to soothe my skin.

Heather Martin (13)
Hethersett High School

I Am A Cat

Under golden moonlight,
Black and white,
Eyes burning bright,
I'm stalking my prey in the darkness of night.

Later I sneak in through an open door
And gently tiptoe across a shiny floor.
I soon lap up the double cream,
Then I glance around for a place to dream.

All curled up in my blanket that's worn,
I purr inside cos it's cosy and warm.
Snuggled in my basket, I'm soft and calm,
But I've one eye open,
Waiting for the next alarm!

Oliver Harvey (12)
Hethersett High School

Lost

I've lost my identity
They've taken it away
I no longer have a name
We're all the same

I've lost my identity
They've taken it away
I'm no longer unique
Nothing different from the rest

I've lost my identity
They've taken it away
I had a happy family
Now they're all gone

I've lost my identity
They've taken it away
I used to have pride
And self-respect

I've lost my identity
They've taken it away
I used to have belongings
All part of me

I've lost my identity
The Nazis took it away
I'm now only a number
Just because I'm a Jew.

Christopher Barnes (12)
Hethersett High School

Identify With Me

Identify with me
my identity.

Look at me,
what do you see?

Two eyes, two ears,
one mouth, one nose.

But

Do you see the years?
Do my feelings show?

Can you see my pain?
Is the hurt there to know?

Do I show my happiness
when I'm bursting inside?

Am I lazy or helpful?
Do I show my pride?

Am I in a good mood
or do I just despair?

Can you see my past
and is my future near?

Can you see my race,
my religion or my faith?

Where are my ancestors?
Have they vanished without trace?

Help me please;
I want to know.

Identify with me
my identity.

Neidín Dunsdon (12)
Hethersett High School

My Identity

You looked at me
And what did you see?
Did you see an old man
Or did you see me?

I hope you saw me,
That would be good,
Because everyone thinks I'm stupid,
Deaf, bad-sighted and a slow walker.

You looked at me
And what did you see?
Did you see a happy man
Or a miserable man in a corner?

A small, broad man,
With tufts of white hair,
A bright man but it doesn't show,
I think that's me.

Paul Baxter (12)
Hethersett High School

The Mystery Creature

The mystery creature
Is tall and broad
Its striking feature
Was the way it roared

It's got a spiky body
And golden wings
Yet it's kind of shoddy
With its rusty rings

Its fluffy tails
Of feathers and fur
Never fails
To cause a stir

Yet weak and scared
Of the light
Its life is bleak
It feeds at night

If you meet this creature
You'll die and burn
And join with nature
To feed the tern.

Jacob Morrison (12)
Hethersett High School

Wilderness

There is a tiger in me . . .
Watching your every move . . .
Waiting for you to make a mistake . . .
And then I'll strike!
This is in me.

There is a fox in me . . .
Always playing tricks . . .
Trying not to be caught . . .
But sometimes you are . . .
This is in me.

There is a crocodile in me . . .
Hiding in the misty feelings of my soul . . .
Camouflaged as a log . . .
But no longer attacks like I do . . .
This is in me.

There is a monkey in me . . .
Saying deep inside my human core,
'I'm not as stupid as I look . . .'
My manual dexterity is second to none . . .
This is inside me.

There is a wolf in me . . .
I rely on my pack . . .
Together nothing is impossible . . .
This is in me.

Although I am the human zoo . . .
The human zoo is me,
Sometimes my cages come undone.

Nick Benfield (13)
Hethersett High School

I Can Be . . .

There is a rabbit in me . . .
I can be friendly or shy,
Tame or wild.
I can run and hide
Or stay and be hugged.
What would I be without
This rabbit in me?

There is a mule in me . . .
I can be helpful or stubborn,
Listen or ignore,
I can be stubborn and not move
Or hardworking and be rewarded,
What would I be without
This mule in me?

There is a monkey in me . . .
I can be cheeky or friendly,
Lively or lazy,
I can be cheeky and throw things
Or friendly and be loved,
What would I be without
This monkey in me?

There is a cat in me . . .
I can be sneaky or cuddly,
Curious or relaxed,
I can be curious and wander anywhere
Or relaxed and don't bother moving,
What would I be without
This cat in me?

All these animals are like a zoo to me,
They control me, they are part of me
And if I lose the key,
All of my animals will escape,
So what would I be if
I lost my key?

James Goddard (13)
Hethersett High School

Wilderness

There is an ox in me . . . unbreakable
during the hardworking day . . .
disobedient when I don't get my way.
I keep this because the wilderness
needs this and I need it too.

There is a barger in me . . . a night-rider
in the dark sky . . . a black and white
creature on legs . . . and a sleepy
bear in the day . . . the wilderness
needs this and I do too.

There is a mouse in me . . . quiet as I go
by my day . . . vicious if I have to be . . .
warm and loving when I need to be . . .
the wilderness needs this and so do I.

I am the zoo but the key has gone
and let out the anger in me.

Brett Waterson (13)
Hethersett High School

The Jungle Within

There is a lion inside me . . . a golden, fur-coated lion . . .
broad shouldered, standing tall.
I pray at night in the dark, scary world.
Sharp teeth rip fresh, new meat.
I got the lion from the jungle within.

There is a mouse within me . . . a tiny, timid mouse.
Backed into a corner, feeling two millimetres tall.
Watching my back all the time, tensing up at every noise.
Not knowing who to and not to trust.
This is the small part of the jungle.

There is a monkey in me . . . cute, cuddly
monkey . . . laid back, friendly.
I stay close within my group but I roam around freely.
I smell intensely around, I smile for attention,
It seems I'm always climbing ladders.
This is from the trees in the jungle.

There is a spider in me . . . a black, delicate
spider . . . hard-working, determined.
I build webs all day, to catch food as well as achievement.
I keep climbing until I get to the top.
This is from below the surface of the jungle.

There is a cage inside me . . . a steel, barred-up cage,
Sometimes I'm a mouse but other times I'm a lion.
I sometimes, accidentally, leave the cage door open
For the whole wide world to see.
This is the jungle inside me, trapped in a cage.

Emma Jermy (13)
Hethersett High School

Wilderness

There is a hyena in me,
Always laughing, never sad, grinning foolishly,
He runs through my thoughts, my mind
And makes me feel happy and silly.
He is me, my sanity, my positivity.

There is an elephant in me,
Standing strong and tall, caring yet threatening,
Always remembering, watching sadly,
Her heart is strong and loving.
She is me, my inner strength, the mother in me.

There is a lion in me,
Tamed to the eye, inside she's burning with anger and fear,
Waiting to strike to be free,
She worries me, I feel for her, she's afraid and betrayed.
She is me, my anger, my sadness and confusion.

There is a sloth in me,
Slow, steady, really quite lazy,
He sits and sits, nothing bothers him,
He watches and listens but does not get involved,
His life doesn't need extra problems.
He is me, my calmness, the diplomat in me.

There is an eagle in me,
Soaring high among the highest mounts
And lowest caverns of my dreams,
She swoops, kills with elegance like a dance.
She is me, the graceful killer, peace of mind, guardian of my soul.

The wilderness is wild, not under my control,
Without them, what would I be?
What is me?
The wilderness is me.

Rachael Cummins (13)
Hethersett High School

The Wilderness

There is a fox in me
It is my cunningness
Always watching
Not making a sound
Waiting for the right time . . .

There is a snake in me
It is my anger
Locked up . . .
And hidden away
Waiting to be let out

There is a cat in me
It is my balance and self control
Relaxed, calm and quiet
Too fast, alert and in control
Without breaking a sweat!

There is a spider in me
It is my determination
Always trying to make a bigger web
And do better than before
So it won't miss a thing

There is a zoo in me
These are inside it
I am the one . . .
Who holds the key
But sometimes I forget to use it.

Tom Cushan-Stubbs (13)
Hethersett High School

This Is Me . . .

There is a rusty lion in me:
It breaks out when something goes wrong,
It goes back in when things calm down,
This is me . . .

There is a soft cat in me:
It's always with me,
It's always nice to people,
This is me . . .

There is a cuddly bear in me:
It's loving and caring,
But it can turn grizzly,
This is me . . .

There is a curious fox in me:
It looks for danger and adventures,
It sneaks up on others,
This is me . . .

All my life,
I've been treated like I'm one person,
But really I'm not . . .

April Cooper (13)
Hethersett High School

The Animals In Me

Inside is a fox
Trapped inside a box
The fox is very cunning
It is good at running
The fox is quiet and sly
Unlike a big, loud fly

Inside me is a cat
Which isn't very fat
Lying very still
Ready to pounce at will
The cat is small and mild
But can turn very wild

Inside me is an owl
Flying on the prowl
The owl is very wise
Observing with his eyes
Sitting on the tree
Watching over me

Inside me is a mouse
Sitting in his house
The mouse is meek and mild
Like me as a child
Hunting round for scraps
Avoiding all the traps

Inside me is a world
Which is nearly all unfurled
If I treat it right
It will help me day and night
But if I leave it be
Then it will start to bother me.

Joseph Ballard (13)
Hethersett High School

Electric Circus

Welcome to my electric circus,
The ringmaster's eyes burn with two blue flames,
I'm a cat in water,
A bird without wings,
A fish on land
And a bee without a hive,
I'm a plug in marionette,
A puppet held by evil strings,
Pulled by malicious two-faced clowns,
Every day we stand round like cattle,
Waiting for the inevitable,
I'm a cat sitting silently,
Scared of my own shadow,
Tears of pain stain my cheeks,
I've been sitting in this cess hole for too long,
Come to my electric circus,
Where the ringmaster tilts his faded hat,
To heartless smiling customers . . .

Alex Paton (14)
Hethersett High School

Wilderness

There is a black panther in me . . . the silent stalker . . .
black fur to blend with the night . . . eyes bright like shining gems . . .
claws of razor-sharp death . . . the snarl of a hunter - I keep the
black panther locked up because the wilderness told me to.

There is a chameleon in me . . . walk of a curious creature . . .
a coat of camouflage for hidden identity . . . eyes dart for seeing all
and a spring of the tongue . . . against prey - I keep the chameleon
on alert . . . for disguise and surprise.

There is a kangaroo in me . . . superb agility . . . from an energetic
jump . . . it's unusual way . . . bringing up offspring . . .
a gentle carer . . . a violent kick-boxer . . .
its aerodynamics - I keep the kangaroo to dart and dance
and entertain me in the burning sun of Australia.

There is a koala in me . . . the sleeper of them all . . .
slow and sluggish . . . carefree and content . . .
soporific and tranquil . . . up in the tree for . . .
food and rest - I need the koala to take me to the sleepy world of
dreams.

These are the animals in me . . . a zoo of zodiac creatures . . .
a menagerie of mystic and mysterious animals . . .
a kingdom of clever and cautious creatures . . .
and like what I am made of . . . I too came from the wilderness . . .
a thing we have no knowledge of except . . . it gave me control
over these animals . . . so I shall make peace . . .
and cause war . . . make new friends . . . and defeat old enemies . . .
with the power of the wilderness.

Andrew Yull (13)
Hethersett High School

There Is A . . .

There is a cat in me: laying still as a statue . . .
Basking in the hot sun, silently,
Prowling as it waits for its prey,
Senses danger and hides . . .
Without this cat I am nothing.

There is an owl in me: swiftly swooping through the night sky . . .
Waiting in the trees in secret,
Preparing its sharp talons ready to kill its prey . . .
Without this owl I am incomplete.

There is a turtle in me: slowly taking its time . . .
To get where it wants,
Nobody can rush it,
In any danger it tucks under its shell . . .
Without this turtle I am empty.

There is a chameleon in me: it blends into the background,
To the naked eye it is invisible,
It waits for the right moment to be seen . . .
Without this chameleon I am only half full.

These are my animals . . .
No one can take them away from me,
Without them I am nothing,
Without them I am incomplete,
Without them I am not me,
They kill me and they protect me,
They cure me and they calm me,
These are my animals . . .
They make me who I am.

Jade Murray (13)
Hethersett High School

What's In Me?

There is a penguin in me . . . a flightless bird
determined to fly . . . but can't . . .
a torpedo in water . . . but has to waddle on land . . .
the golden and white colours upon its breast
that will never fade.

There is a white Bengal tiger in me . . .
fast . . . rare . . . and lying so still ready to pounce . . .
black and white . . . the colours simple . . . but confusing . . .
the world's a mystery.

There is a monkey in me . . . cheeky and
intelligent . . . small but strong . . .
most time spent above the ground . . .
leaping from tree to tree . . . as though on land . . .
but in air . . . they are free.

There is a tarantula in me . . .
humongous . . . hairy and chilling . . .
all eyes focussed on the prey . . .
its web glittering in the dew . . .
spinning silk around the helpless prey . . .
getting more hungry . . .
and this tarantula came to me from the wilderness.

Pippa Griffith-Jones (13)
Hethersett High School

The Wilderness

There is a cat in me . . .
Yawning and sleeping in front of the fire . . .
Running then jumping off roofs . . .
Hunting and murdering young animals . . .
I cannot live with this, it is my personality.

There is a peacock in me . . .
Grooming and washing its tail . . .
Fanning out its tail, to show the colours of the rainbow . . .
I cannot live with this, it is what I look like.

There is a hippo in me . . .
Languishing in the water forever on end . . .
Sleeping in the sun or under the trees . . .
I cannot live without this, it is who I am.

There is a monkey in me . . .
Jumping and laughing with my friends . . .
Being cheeky to my mum and dad and having a laugh
and a joke . . .
I cannot live with this, it is my cheekiness.

Katie Jeffries (13)
Hethersett High School

Wilderness!

There is a snake in me . . . slithering dangerously in the grass . . .
brilliant forked tongue, ready to pierce its red-hot fangs in its prey . . .
such an elegant creature but also arrogant . . .
the wilderness gave them to me.

There is a chipmunk in me . . . stunning, smooth skin -
very athletic, quick, ready to pounce . . . perfectly shaped . . .
cute, loveable yet fierce and vicious . . .
the wilderness gave them to me.

There is a panther in me . . . lying in the grass ready to pounce,
never gives up, elegant, sleek, majestic, gorgeous skin,
golden yellow eyes, fast as lightning . . .
the wilderness gave them to me.

There is an elephant in me . . . as smart as the world old . . .
as strong as an ox, never forgets anything . . .
the wilderness gave them to me.

These are my animals, they help me and hurt me,
if they get released, I get released . . .
the wilderness gave them to me.

Daniel Arden (13)
Hethersett High School

The Wilderness

There is an iguana in me . . .
hiding around in trees,
avoiding all threats and enemies . . .
quietly hiding too and seeking shelter . . .
then it makes no rash decisions
or does anything stupid . . .
I keep this iguana as it's the sensible part of me . . .
and the wilderness gave this to me
and I will not let it go.

There is a bird in me . . .
it likes to travel around and to see the world . . .
it protects over its young and family . . .
always alert and watching . . .
the wilderness told me to keep this.

There is a bear in me . . .
a mouth and a nose . . .
to eat and breathe . . .
it sees something it wants
and will not stop until it gets what it wants . . .
the bear is from the wilderness
and the wilderness told me I needed it.

There is a dolphin in me . . .
intelligence and bravery . . .
helping people in need . . .
elegance and speed . . .
showing off my skill,
the wilderness said I would be nothing
without this, so I kept it.

Sam Fryer (13)
Hethersett High School

Wilderness

There is a lion in me . . . big lungs for
a very loud roar . . . sleepy, working, hunting
for prey, determination, fierce,
could you survive without this?

There is a fish in me . . . a swordfish,
sharpness, always alert, a born hunter . . .
and in the opposite . . . a goldfish, floating around . . .
relaxed inside a glass open bowl, the freedom . . .
could you survive without this?

There is a bird in me . . . a bald eagle . . .
searching with telescopic eyes . . .
swoop in and grab . . . the fresh meat of a rabbit . . .
and in the opposite . . . a swift . . . it's all in the name,
nimble and quick . . . searching for wriggly worms,
flying in the freedom of the skies . . .
could you survive without this?

There is a chameleon in me . . . you can't
see unless you look hard among the leaves . . .
blending in . . . easily unseen, he doesn't rush . . .
too fast and he will be taken by predators . . .
slinky, sly . . . could you live without this?

Arron Smith (13)
Hethersett High School

The First Kiss

Amongst the darkness of the night,
A couple rowed in a town flat,
Until both gave up the evening light,
And alone travelled in the shadows.

In the blackness of an alley,
Two shaded figures came together,
And under the world's greatest tally,
Gave the night's world its first kiss.

Later that night the couple met,
Again and again to argue,
With never a soul to yet let,
The troubled truth unfold.

Who were they then those figures,
That met that chilly night?
With no soul to pull what triggers,
To that rowing couple?

Ah, my friend can't you see,
With such charms around you?
Say those figures were you and me,
What would become of that?

Abigail Robinson (13)
Hethersett High School

The Wilderness

There is a cat in me . . . curious and interested . . .
climbing high among the leaves . . . crazy ideas . . .
doing as it pleased, coming and going . . .
wandering the dark outside . . . padding softly . . .
crouching silently . . . waiting to pounce . . .
a smooth criminal.

There is a butterfly in me . . . flitting around in
my head with ideas . . . making the most of its
short life . . . planning no future . . . spreading its
wings to the summer sun . . . showing off admiral
colours . . . sipping nectar from flowers passed
because the wilderness has given me the
butterfly and I keep it because the wilderness says so.

There is a dolphin in me . . . smiling, keeping a
secret . . . swimming and leaping gracefully . . .
piercing the water without so much as a splash . . .
having no cares or worries . . . leading ships
through stormy seas . . . sensing safety and
danger . . . knowing.

There is a raven in me . . . flying high, swooping
low . . . sleek, black feathers . . . harsh voice calling
out . . . alone in moorland crags, along rocky
coasts gliding majestically . . . a powerful beak . . .
a mysterious corvus corax - the wilderness
gave me the raven and the wilderness will
not let it go.

Aislinn Tully (13)
Hethersett High School

The Wilderness

There is a giraffe in me . . . tall with
beady eyes . . . looking out for danger.
I am a giraffe . . . and that's how . . .
the wilderness made me.

There is a mouse in me . . . scuttling
around . . . quick footwork always comes
in handy when escaping.
I am a mouse and that is how . . .
the wilderness created me.

There is a rhino in me . . . the temper
sometimes is expressed . . . when released
it is wild . . . the rhino I have grabbed is
of the wilderness.

There is a meerkat in me . . . extremely
wide eyesight . . . the meerkat looks out
for its friends . . .
the wilderness gave this animal to me.

The animals in me are trying to escape . . .
but I keep them in . . . I only sometimes
let a little bit of the animal out.

Stuart Holland (14)
Hethersett High School

Identity Poem

S ensible and
A rtistic, very
M odern and
A greeable. I am also
N ice and
T hirteen years old
H appy and
A dmirable

E nthusiastic
D own to earth and
W ary of what's
A round her
R easonable and
D reamy
S uperstar.

Samantha Edwards (13)
Hethersett High School

Who Are You?

'Who are you?' you ask
Whilst looking at me,
Well the answer is
Explained quite simply,
I am myself
And nobody else
And will continue forever to be.

Kaily Keenaghan (13)
Hethersett High School

Wilderness

There is a bear in me . . . rough and wild . . .
lashing out . . . fierce and angry and this bear
stays in the wilderness because I say.

There is a bull in me . . . raging . . . furious . . . charging
never ceasing . . . never rests - this bull is
with me and shall always be.

There is a horse in me . . . wild and untamed . . . free
afraid . . . rearing up against the hunting predator -
this horse is mine and it will never leave.

There is a wild cat in me . . . with sharp claws . . .
hunting . . . waiting . . . relentless in the red-hot blood of the
night - this wild cat belongs to the wilderness and the
wilderness belongs to me.

I am the keeper of the zoo
and sometimes I forget to lock the cages!

Michael Sanders (13)
Hethersett High School

Lu Bu (The Mighty)

The mightiest warrior on the land
Goes into battle with his golden spear
No one will live if you are his enemy and
His skill with a weapon might kill with fear

He lives with no ally and nobody, the fact
That he trains 24/7, will make the enemy flee
You will die by the certain impact
He hates everyone, especially team Wei

So you know the truth
That Lu Bu is the best
He asks, 'Who dares challenge thee?'
Who will die next?

Matt Newson (12)
Hethersett High School

Wilderness

There is a squirrel in me . . . a flying squirrel . . .
shy and minding its own business . . .
collecting nuts, collecting information . . . ready to put to great
use at any point . . . sharp claws . . . wary, not wanting
to be caught out . . . not wanting to be captured . . .
scurrying away from danger with lightning-quick reactions.
The wilderness gave me this tender animal of nature . . .
and I do not want to let it go.

There is an elephant in me . . . kind and magnificent . . . highly
intelligent . . . usually human friendly . . . bad tempered and strong . . .
never forgetting the people who mistreated me . . . waiting
for the person I hate, that used me . . .
waiting for the chance to get my own back - to lash out
on someone . . . anyone.
The wilderness gave me this great beast and I do not want to let it go.

There is a dolphin in me . . . living around others . . . very friendly . . .
high intelligent . . . gentle and delightful.
The wilderness gave me this gift and I do not want to let it go.

There is a dog in me . . . a man's best friend . . .
ferocious . . . barking . . . well trained. The wilderness gave me
this animal and I do not want to let it go.

There is rhino in me . . . definite and stout . . . conscious of
everything . . . humans always at them for one of their qualities . . .
excellent sense of smell . . . rare, almost extinct . . . waiting
to break out of its shell, to attack . . .
experienced . . . charge and grab hold of anything suspicious.
The wilderness gave me this wonder and I do not want to let it go.

I have all these great creatures. The wilderness is to thank.
Usually I keep these animals controlled and under my skin,
but when they break out, it can have a weird, weird effect on me
and anything nearby. It could be so nice, so magnificent,
but if you catch *my* animals in a mood, or if you mistreat them,
it can have lethal consequences.

Christopher Holmes (13)
Hethersett High School

Wilderness

There is a wasp in me; this is my anger
cooped up, caged in a corner, buzzing
and humming threateningly.
Waiting to be released at the right time . . .
no one could survive without this.

There is a rainforest vine in me; this is my determination
always growing, upwards towards the sun,
past the dark trees of failure,
to the sky, to the sun, never ceasing . . .
no one could survive without this . . .

There is a cat in me; this controls my movement
with lightning-fast reaction,
lazy, laid back slumber, to alert, vigilant concentration
in three short seconds . . .
no one could survive without this . . .

There is a fox in me; this is my cunning
watching everything with beady eyes,
darting here and there, missing nothing,
always ready for the unexpected . . .
no one could survive without this . . .

There are the animals of the world . . .
and of me. They control me and obey me,
they help me and hurt me. They are me.
I cannot survive without them.

Edward Knights (13)
Hethersett High School

The Wilderness

There is a mouse in me . . .
scuttling inside the skirting boards . . .
toing and froing . . . dreading the pounce.

There is a cat in me . . .
straying along the dusty lanes . . .
tail on end . . .
always returning to its owner's gentle hand.

There is a bull in me . . .
spurred on by the red flag . . .
turning its fearsome horns at a butterfly's flutter . . .
daring anyone to brave its temper.

There is a mole in me . . .
clawing along a dark passage . . .
feeling its way . . . blind to the colours
of the world outside its eyelids.

Inside me is the patter of a paw . . .
the sharpness of a horn . . .
the blindness of an eye and the prickling of a tail . . .
each to its own . . . each obeying the mind cloud
towering over it.

Naomi Smith (14)
Hethersett High School

Wilderness

There is a snake in me . . . my slickly look makes
your hair stand on end . . . I slide past unaware, then
suddenly I appear . . . I hisssssss, you hear, you
fear . . . I keep my snake locked away so you don't
feel the fear . . . when I fang you with my venom.

There is an owl in me . . . my eyes so bright, I hunt my
prey through the night . . . I glide around so peaceful . . .
life is busy, head turning round and round . . .
so don't make too much sound . . . I love to let my owl free,
I go to sleep, oh so peaceful . . . can't you see?

There is an elephant in me . . . I never, never forget, so lie
you'll regret . . . I thud through my kingdom swinging
and swaying, I am the leader . . . always rising to
the challenge, having to fight my rivals . . . I would
never let my elephant out, people would shout,
I would scare them and myself!

There is a bear in me . . . I'm strong and intelligent, these
are my lethal weapons . . . there is two sides to me, I
scare my prey and rivals, but love my kind and family . . .
I am quite lazy so sleep in winter . . . I could not let
my bear run loose because I could not trust my dangerous side.

If I was to let all my animals wild, I would have
mixed emotions and my head would be sore of the hassle,
not to mention others' heads!

Louis Le-May (13)
Hethersett High School

Wilderness

There is a tiger in me . . . teeth as sharp as a dagger
to tear animals to shreds, to prance and to hunt for fresh flesh,
I keep the tiger with me at all times because the wilderness will not let it go.

There is a rabbit in me . . . jumpy, bouncy legs to jump through
the grass with the watery, crunchy lettuce,
I hop . . . I skip . . . and I jump.

There is a bat in me . . . I come alive at night,
I send signals that no one else can hear,
I flutter around graveyards in the dead of the night,
I got this from the wilderness and I don't want to let it go.

There is a cheetah in me . . . fast and furious,
I rage with anger,
I wait quietly then I . . . prance at my prey,
Then I run, run, run away.

All of these amazing creatures are inside me,
sometimes the bad creatures escape and take control over me,
I get so angry and upset, so I burst with anger,
they do this because . . . I tell them to!

Amy Gawthorpe (13)
Hethersett High School

The Wilderness

I have a wild horse in me . . .
Galloping over wild plains
Spirit soaring high . . . roaming free
I keep it because the wilderness gave it to me
And I will not let it go

There is a butterfly in me . . .
Flitting around the flowers
Basking in the sun
Soon disappearing in the colder days

I have a turtle in me . . .
Plodding on determined
Never stopping until he's finished

I have a rabbit in me
Skitty and scatty
Happy as can be . . . running and jumping
Mad in the summer months

Sometimes the animals within me go out of control
The horse will gallop too fast, the butterfly will not bask in the sun
And the turtle will be too determined
And they will break through the cages.

Lisa Blanchflower (13)
Hethersett High School

Animals I Am

I am a snake,
Sly, fast and always watching,
Ready for any challenge,
I hold this thing for fear of its escape.

I am a tiger,
Grand, bold and always on form,
Ready for any attack,
I hold this thing for fear of its escape.

I am a shark,
Swift, smart and always on the move,
Ready for any adventure,
I hold this thing for fear of its escape.

I am a rhino,
Headstrong, stubborn and angry,
Ready to breach control,
I hold this thing for fear of its escape.

I hold all these beasts,
Unbalanced, changing and a great part of my existence,
All of them horrific alone,
Which is why I must not let them free.

But all these beasts
Lose control
And can sometimes
Break the fences.

Sam Willis (13)
Hethersett High School

Wilderness

Sometimes I feel there is a bird in me . . .
It wants to be free but it must never escape . . .
It stays calm and collected but always aware . . .
For me she watches . . .
This was a gift . . .
A gift from the wilderness.

Sometimes I feel there is a tiger in me . . .
Tame and happy . . .
Until she is disturbed then she flips . . .
She howls and growls . . .
Then when she has let off all her steam . . .
It's back to tame old tiger . . .
This was a gift . . .
A gift from the wilderness.

Sometimes I feel there is a fish in me . . .
Oblivious to everything and everyone around . . .
Always in an ocean of its own . . .
Can never think what to say or do . . .
Can't concentrate . . .
This was a gift . . .
A gift from the wilderness.

Sometimes I feel there is an elephant in me . . .
Big, strong and fearless . . .
Always the leader of the gang not the follower . . .
Never forgetting . . .
This was a gift . . .
A gift from the wilderness.

Sometimes I feel like I am just me . . .
The gates to the zoo are closed . . .
I hold the key . . .
Those gifts I accept gratefully . . .
And vow to keep . . .
Those gifts from the wilderness.

Jessica Brown (13)
Hethersett High School

Whose Reflection Is That?

I looked in the mirror,
What did I see?
Not him or her,
No, just me.

The same cheery smile
And the long brown hair,
The same personality
And who always cares.

My full, thick lips
And my shiny skin,
My trendy clothes
And my light tanned skin.

I looked in the mirror,
Guess what I did see?
I saw the girl, who I always see,
Yes, that's right, just the same old me!

Kelly Spaul (12)
Hethersett High School

Unexplained Kurt Cobain

Dirty blond hair,
Bullet-blue eyes,
A musical saviour locked in a heart-shaped box.

Love stole the box,
She invited Death in,
Music revolution
Brought to a stop,
At his drug-stained death.

Our unexplained Kurt Cobain.

Roz Attwood (12)
Hethersett High School

Wilderness!

There is a tiger in me . . . claws and sharp teeth . . .
always alert . . . confident and fierce . . . free and powerful . . .
the wilderness gave it to me and it won't let it go.

There is a monkey in me . . . happy and loud . . .
bouncy and mad . . . hairy and mischievous . . .
I keep the monkey because the wilderness needs me to.

There is a fish in me . . . gentle and calm . . .
colourful and quiet . . . open to swim wherever, whenever
in the deep sea . . . sometimes not knowing what to do . . .
but I keep this animal because the wilderness tells me to.

There is a dolphin in me . . . that loves to play . . .
have fun and muck about . . . it has predators . . .
angry and hungry . . . looking for food . . . planning to kill . . .
the wilderness gave the dolphin to me and I have to protect it.

There is an egg in me . . . full of all the animals . . .
it is from the wilderness . . . where the animals come from . . .
where they begin . . . where they are formed . . .
it is a connection with me and the wilderness . . .
it gives me the animals . . . I keep the animals . . .
I look after the animals and the wilderness looks after me!

Imogen Ranger (13)
Hethersett High School

Myself Poem

I looked in the mirror
And what did I see?
Not white, not pink
But just me
With big diamond eyes
And white sparkly teeth
And curly, brown hair as far as can be

Yes I looked in the mirror
What did I see?
A box full of emotion
Happy but nervy
Only she holds the key

Yes, tall, dark and handsome
With luscious lips
And a bright, shiny smile
That can't wait to be kissed

I looked in the mirror
Who did I see?
That guy I know
That guy's only me!

Grace Adams (13)
Hethersett High School

Black Man

I looked in the mirror
What did I see?
Ali G wannabe
Looking back at me

Coal-black face
With big, bright eyes
Sparkling white teeth
What a surprise

Yes, I looked in the mirror
What did I see?
A big black man
Smelling pleasantly

Short, broad nose
Full thick lips
Curly black hair
And dark brown eyes

You may see black
You may see white
But you'll never see the inside of me.

Daniel Clements (13)
Hethersett High School

In The Mirror

I looked in the mirror,
What did I see?
Not tall, not short,
But only me!
With big, dazzling eyes
And pearly-white teeth
And blonde hair as far as the sea!

Yes, I looked in the mirror,
What did I see?
I saw a lad
Who's dear to me.
He's tall and dark,
With bright blue eyes
And really cool to see.

I looked in the mirror,
What did I see?
Not white, not black,
But someone like me,
Who's really kind and fun to be
And will be your friend for eternity.

Yes, I looked in the mirror
For one last time,
What did I see?
Not tall, not short,
Not black, not white,
But only someone
Who's little old *me!*

Jade Shannon (13)
Hethersett High School

Wilderness

There is a killer whale in me
waiting to catch a wave into shore
the ability to swim well, fast and far
the wilderness gave it to me and I won't let it go

There is a lion in me ready for a meat feast
anger boiling up inside of me
the wilderness gave this to me and I cannot let it go

There is a hawk in me, skilful and sharp
I glide through the air and scan the air below
as graceful as the air

There is a dolphin in me, calm, quick, clever and kind
the wilderness gave me this and I will not let it go

I look after all these animals inside me
and I won't let them go
apart from the lion that gets away from me.

Sam Spaul (13)
Hethersett High School

An African Scene

An African scene
from a dried-out plain
with a warthog
scuttling by.

An African scene
with a rounded
beating sun
and no place to hide.

An African scene
with the anticipation
of a zebra about to be
taken out by a skilful
speedy cheetah.

An African scene
with a beating sun
and a meal for a cheetah
with a warthog scuttling by.

Sabrina Johnson (11)
Hethersett Old Hall School

Who, Where, What, Why, When

She was a little girl in bed,
Who lived upon a water shed,
But one day she bashed her little head
And made it so very raw and red.

She had a father whose name was Ted,
In a factory he worked making lead,
One day a fairy came up to her and said,
'I wonder if today your dog has been fed?'
The girl again became very red,
'No, I have not fed Fred,
I'll go and get him some mouldy bread.'
'OK,' said the fairy, 'be careful where you tread.'
The girl went down, but instead,
She went on a ride on her moped,
She forgot to put a helmet on her head,
She fell to the floor and soon was dead.

Shelley Forsdyke (11)
Hethersett Old Hall School

A Granny Poem

She smiles as she sees me,
Her false teeth clatter as she talks.
She struggles in her wheelchair,
Her dementia grows even longer.

She has two white hairs on her chin.
Her heavy jewellery hangs on her neck.
She chooses which glasses Poppa wears.
She chooses which hat she should wear.

She worries about her handbag.
Some days she looks so solemn,
She asks so many questions,
She doesn't eat much.

She goes to bed at 6 o'clock at night.
I have something to admit,
This is Granny.

Emma Hopkins (11)
Hethersett Old Hall School

The Postbox

When I was young, I always thought
The postbox was alive!
The big, red, scary letter-eater,
I was scared to go close,
Even to put my hand inside.

When I was older, I was more curious,
'What did those letters mean, Mum?'
ER were the letters I traced.
I loved to stick my hand inside and almost get it stuck.
I'd watch the big red van go by, admiring it as it went.

Now, in my 40s, I drive the big red truck,
I have a set of keys so my hand doesn't get stuck.
I watch the kids, but they don't marvel at me.
Instead they stop in back alleys
And spray them with graffiti.

Laura Woods (11)
Hethersett Old Hall School

The Autumn Dreary Weather

The autumn leaves are falling upon the damp ground
The sky is forming a very black cloud
The leaves are coloured red, orange, yellow and brown
How beautiful they are, who can frown?

I love the air so fresh and moist
The feeling of a healing voice
I want to play among the leaves
Jump and fall and get mud on my knees

The rain is falling upon my hand
And the sunshine's burnish gold upon my land
An angry cry of a violent storm
The leaves are hurling from dust to dawn.

Joanna Phillips (13)
Norwich High School for Girls

Busyness

Busyness is the M25,
The M25 is rush hour,
Rush hour on a freezing cold day,
A freezing cold day when it's snowing,
When it's snowing so hard you can't see where you're going.

Busyness is thousands of ants scurrying about,
Scurrying to find food,
To find food to put in their food stores,
Their food stores for when times get hard,
When times get hard and food is scarce.

Busyness is the shops in the city,
The shops in the city on late night shopping night,
Late night shopping night when the people look like ants,
Like ants scurrying to get the bargains,
The bargains on clothes, not on tasty morsels.

Katie Lister (11)
Norwich High School for Girls

The China Doll

I longed to take Emily from the shelf,
Touch her rosy cheeks,
Porcelain, like velvet.
I'd held her once, secretly,
The dress, red velvet, exquisite, like royalty,
Cream suede slippers on delicate toes,
Lovely ringlets perfectly placed as if fixed to her crimson frills,
Look so serene, that touch might shatter,
To hold her, warm her stone-cold body, bring her to life,
Out of reach,
Untouchable.

Bethany Copping (13)
Norwich High School for Girls

Changing Faces

She was my friend,
But what is a friend?
Funny, kind, clever mind,
Qualities like these, oh, she had them,
A friendship lasted so long,
Where did I go wrong?

The spite creeps slowly,
I could not see,
That who I had adored
Would be taken from me,
A brick wall encased
Her once giggling heart,
The stabs of scorn
That wrenched us apart.

The insecurity in the knowledge
That she was my friend today,
That the sun would shine brightly,
Or if it would thunder and rain.
So she was my fair-weather friend,
My friendship that was feigned,
But then the harsh wind blew too hard
And her thunder face remained.

Her scorn, her sarcasm,
Hard, harsh wit
Infected those around her,
A group into which I did not fit,
Where brewed a boredom and a spite,
To use most generously,
To use a most hurtful bite,
To take it out on me.

My mama, she really tried,
When I arrived home from school,
I lay in her arms and cried,
And just repeated, 'Why?
Why is it me that they reject?
Where was it that I went wrong?
How is it that she them all infect?
Don't just tell me to be strong.
Does it matter if I went to bed at eight?
Who cares who *Greenday* were?
How could my best friend
Now me hate?' Those weeks
Became a blur.

I simply remember hating break,
I wanted to stay indoors,
Hated seeing her on the field,
Whilst I sat alone on a bench,
Hated seeing their tight-knit group,
I felt my throat and knuckles clench.

So what if I had ginger hair?
So what if I was good at English?
Why should they, when I wouldn't dare?
I didn't want to be alone.

But now that's gone,
A mist of a memory
And I've finally found the confidence
To be myself.
This school may pressurise,
May have no boys,
But the girls are lovely – no doubt.

So when you choose your friends,
Choose them carefully,
I've got my best friends now
And I know that they'll stand by me.

Jessica Staufenberg (13)
Norwich High School for Girls

Lonely Girl

I'm so lonely,
Spent so much time alone,
Got no friends to turn to,
No place to call my home.

Since you left me,
Stranded me in tears,
I won't forget you
And how you made me fear.

You took all my money,
Beat me, that's not right,
I couldn't talk up to you,
Didn't know how to fight.

You left me so numb,
I can never love again
And all I feel is pain,
Day after day after day after day.

I'm so lonely,
You made me feel so numb,
I can't forgive you,
For everything you've done.
Why does it still hurt me so bad?
Why can't I sleep the pain away?
Why can't I turn off the tap that makes these tears flow every day?

I'm so lonely,
You made me feel so dumb,
Now you've got me questioning,
Is it my fault this begun?

Everyone looks down on me,
The ice is wearing thin,
At first I felt worthless,
Now I might explode from within.

Oh, I'm so lonely,
Spent so much time alone,
Got no friends to turn to,
No place to call my home.

Stephanie Fare (13)
Norwich High School for Girls

Beauty Of The Forest

I can hear the flowing rushing water,
Though I'm sitting where the water is still as stone
My eyes open slowly under my wet lashes
I'm held close in a protective embrace, warm to his heart
I can hear the wind call an unknown name
The sun rising in the east waking all that live
The leaves become alive with the wind swirling around us waking
Us from our warm slumber.
My eyes take in the beauty of the forest
The heavy grey rocks are covered in the soft green moss
I look at the beauty of the water and see my image reflected
The leaves of the oak and the birches rustle trying to break
Free from its holder
The roots of the trees are not hidden but break free
From its binding with the Earth
An intricate pattern of swirls and lines lay on the bark
Of these sacred trees
A layer of soft bedding made of fallen leaves lay on the ground
Hiding those that will never return
The forest is but one colour, green in different shade
The sound of the living come alive, but the spirits are still heard
The day has dawned
The blazing sun has left the deep blue sky to sleep behind the
Hollow green trees and darkness is spreading its wings.
To bring the black of the night
To leave me with just the sounds of darkness
And the endless diamond stars in the sky
Beautiful the forest may be but you may never see the
Same place again.

Chamaale Dooldeniya (13)
Norwich High School for Girls

William

The new horse, William,
Now comes off the lorry,
I'm getting very, very excited,
I just can't wait to ride him on the track,
I put on his back, a brand new saddle
And on his head, a shiny new bridle,
He is now very keen,
As I pull down the stirrups and sit in the saddle,
It feels very weird because he is so big,
Totally different to my little pony,
As I trot down the lane,
A tear falls down my cheek,
But not because I am sad, just very, very happy,
We set off onto the track and start cantering,
Cantering as fast as the wind,
His ears are forward, he is pleased,
I pull on the reins just ever so slightly,
He comes back to a trot and then a walk,
Back down the lane
And into the silent yard,
I had so much fun and can't wait to ride him again,
Now I have my new horse, William.

Hari Milburn (13)
Norwich High School for Girls

My Bed!

I'm awoken every morning,
With that feeling in my heart,
Please don't take me away from it,
Please don't force us apart.

I was snugly and warm,
Like a joey in its pouch,
I love lying silent and still,
I don't want to move about!

I stroll towards the bathroom,
We were separated once more,
I concentrated hard on opening my eyes
And lifting each foot off the floor.

I dress myself lazily,
I style my hair,
But I want to be back in my dreamland,
I'd give anything to be back there!

It's a weird sensation,
I'm speeding up,
I'm gradually reaching my goal,
To leave the house, get on my bus
And arrive at school as a whole.

Sometimes I don't achieve it,
I get to school half awake,
I want to return to my favourite place,
How long is this day going to take?

I feel like a dog deprived of its dinner,
Like a child torn from her toy,
But soon I meet others, who feel the same way,
They've also been deprived of their morning joy!

We soon start laughing, chatting and shouting,
It's weird how you can just forget,
One minute you'd give everything to be somewhere else,
But you couldn't care less the next!

Faye Franklin (13)
Norwich High School for Girls

Abuse

I see closed doors,
Doors and windows,
Windows are glass,
Glasses smashed,
She smashed my face,
Face, my mother said was everything,
Everything is black,
Black is night,
Night is sleep,
Sleep, I get none,
None, I feel no love, none exists,
Exist, something my mother said I shouldn't.

Me, it all comes down to me.

I can't escape,
I'm lost in my thoughts,
My mother screaming, hitting, killing,
But I get there first,
I'm not last in my thoughts,
I'm lost in my own death,
Death that I made.

Me, it all comes down to me.

Hannah Hedegard (14)
Norwich High School for Girls

Thorn Of Beauty

Pure perfection,
Exaggerated beauty,
Eyes like dreamy oceans,
Mysterious and deep.
Skin; silky smooth and golden . . .
Like the sun, untouchable.
A mortal lays a finger,
On this being so unnatural, unchallenged
And is burned.
For a creature so exquisite,
Could only taint one's dirty hand,
With its liquid fantasy.
Any man with love of life,
Would avoid this shallow mind,
For she won't be, can't be pure perfection,
When no truth lies, within pure lies
And eyes that hypnotise,
These eyes would compromise,
Her so-called perfect mind.
How can 'Beauty' be not ugly called,
When this lady's beauty is like a rose?
So sweet it is to smell, to see,
But its irresistible apparent beauty causes pain to touch,
As sharp green thorns do penetrate the skin
And mimic the piercing of a poor fool's heart,
As the killer reels him in.

Nadia Hagen (13)
Norwich High School for Girls

A Night Out With Your Mates

Flying through the window,
Your life before your eyes.
Memories you couldn't remember,
Memories of lies.
Life was so easy,
Before you were here,
Don't waste your last breath,
On stopping your last tear.
Never ever again,
You won't go out with your friend.
Never get to do your thing,
It's turned another bend.
The glass is cutting at your throat,
Your eye smashed on the dashboard
And no one is alive to comfort you,
Or hear your last words echo into the dark night as you crash
Into the car in front.
No one to see.
No one to know.
No one to feel.
No one to hear.
No one around at all.
You are all alone in the middle of a road,
Watching the drunken fool who was driving
Roll stupidly to the floor with a thump.
How stupid indeed.

Laura Earl (13)
Norwich High School for Girls

She Has Awakened

The trees are sagging under bows laden with amber fruits,
And above the orchard a mist hangs, dazzling as the first rays
of morning touch this waking world.
But time has struck an icy gong and every living thing shudders
at the sound,
For they know: She has awakened.

Pale grey eyes like frozen stones
watch out under jet-black lashes;
Where her fingers stray to touch
leaves curl and fall like ashes.

Snow-white face and icy lips
of deadly beauty tell;
With age-old magic she has learnt
to cast this final spell.

Where her feet fall cold descends
and grips the earth in frost.
All thought of life before soon fades,
to darkness all is lost.

Like midnight sky her cloak is made
and from its darkest folds
Sing bitter-sweet the stars of all
that their great memory holds.

And so she passes like a dream
and blissful sleep delivers;
But at the other side there's light
and gifts from other givers.

Rebecca Williams (14)
Norwich High School for Girls

I Am Alone

I am alone, alone am I,
Though I am not alone,
Trapped in my mind,
A devil seeks
To destroy my soul,
Forever, forever.

It controls my feelings,
My thoughts and deeds.
I cannot control
My own mind,
For the Devil has it all,
Forever, forever.

No one knows
And no one understands.
No one can see my torment.
If only they knew,
If only they understood,
Forever, forever.

But I am alone,
With no one to care,
No one to say, 'Don't worry.'
No one to take the pain,
The knowledge of that Devil,
Forever, forever.

Janet Yarham (13)
Norwich High School for Girls

Supper Tomorrow

For supper tomorrow,
I don't know what we'll have,
For supper tomorrow we might have anything,
It could be chips,
It could be beans,
It could be cheese on toast,
Just don't ask me.

It could be salads,
It could be pizza,
It could be fresh hot pancakes,
But for all I know it could be all three,
That is the reason you should not ask me.

It could be home-made,
It could be a freezer meal,
It could be a takeaway,
You never know, it might be blue,
So please, please, please,
I have not got a clue.

It could be a quick and simple meal,
It could be quite complex,
Or maybe a just-right meal,
A simply *delicious meal!*

Celia Cooper (13)
Norwich High School for Girls

King Of The Jungle

Many people say as fact
That lions always rule the pack,
But I completely disagree,
The tiger is the king for me.

Nothing is so fearless, yet such a rarity,
The tiger is a symbol, which deserves some dignity,
Its presence is majestic as it roams the jungle track,
If it's hunted to extinction, they'll only wish it back.

Fire eyes, striped coat you cannot see,
The jungle is its territory,
It reigns the land without a fight,
Only man can kill this sight.

Its stunning coat as fluffy as snow,
As bright and vibrant as a glow,
Its dashing colours both thick and thin,
Pouncing all over its wonderful skin.

This solitary animal, beautiful by sight,
Resting by day, hunting by night,
Waiting for that perfect moment,
Making sure there's no repent.

Undisputed king of its domain,
Nothing in nature can cause it pain,
No challenger will ever be,
The tiger is the king for me.

Charlotte Cumby (13)
Norwich High School for Girls

The Great Blue Yonder

The cold wind blew into my face as I shut the door with a bang,
I pulled my coat tightly around me and blew hot air into my hands.
I scuffed my shoes along the road thinking of the days to come,
Riding along the beach, eating ice creams, spending all day in
the warm golden sun.
I stepped out into the road, lost in an old memory,
Oh why didn't I listen when Mum told me to stop, look, listen, see?
But I didn't see the car looming close, skidding on its way.
I hadn't realised, I hadn't known that I was going to die this day.
The pain cut into me as hard as it could go.
I started to scream as hard as I could, shouting, 'No, no!'
The torture suddenly left me as I lay there on the cold ice.
I asked God quietly why I had to pay the awful price.
The voices around me grew fainter and fainter,
As I wandered off into the great blue yonder.

Alice Payton (13)
Norwich High School for Girls

Darkness

I look around but what I know,
The appearances of shapes don't show,
My eyes won't work, I cannot see,
This darkness creeping up on me.

I try to run, I try to hide,
From the darkness deep inside,
I trip, I stumble, I try to flee,
The darkness catching up with me.

I except my fate, I am now blind,
Beautiful colours I can't find,
Orange, purple, pink and blue,
Has the darkness yet found you?

Emma Leighton (12)
Norwich High School for Girls

The Alleyway

The foreboding alley is as ominous as the hours of darkness,
A dying street lamp stutters like a firefly drowning in mist.
Molluscs set off on their hazardous expedition,
Inaudibly interlacing leaves.
A voyage to security, refuge and harmony.

On the left,
Foliage sighs like a dying, tortured, mythological dragon
Of a spiritual golden dimension.
Latent on the sodden earth in vain,
A deceased rose like a barbed and crippled being.
Threatening provinces loom ahead,
A coiling, spiralling wind summons you onwards.

To the right,
On the lustrous moonlit wall,
A shaft of crystal beam snaps the frozen atmosphere.
Antagonistic alley cats spit and stare.
Gliding through aerated matted sludge,
Tunnelling through choking vegetation,
Worms sashay like sinuous waterways.

It commences to rain.
Rain resembling lamenting tears.

Glacial footsteps.
Casting a blanket of frosted glass.
The dawn has divulged her beauty.
The mortals veil themselves skilfully.
Alley cats slink off.
The opening natural world chants.

Abigail Parker (13)
Norwich High School for Girls

Nothing

People are running, tired, hungry and distraught,
Chemical gas fills the lungs of little children,
Animals lay dead, tongues hanging out of their furry heads.

People dying, children crying, what did they do to deserve this?

Schools and homes fall in seconds, so quickly,
All hope is gone just in one day,
Mental damage forever and ever.

People dying, children crying, what did they do to deserve this?

Terror, fighting, death, hell has been forced into their lives,
Bodies are laid dead, silent for miles around,
Blood bleeds out of every little soul.

People dying, children crying, what did they do to deserve this?

Darkness surrounds them even in day,
Bombs are going off all the time. Will it end?
Trapped forever in a world worse than death.

People dying, children crying, what did they do to deserve this?

Nothing,
Nothing,
Nothing at all.

Sarah Gardner (12)
Norwich High School for Girls

Autumn

It is coming, I know it is.

I can feel it on my cheeks,
I can see it on the ground,
I can hear it through the trees,
I can smell it outside and in the kitchen,
I can't speak its language but I can say its name.

I can sense it coming.

It rolls over hills
And rustles through trees,
Pulling leaves down onto the ground bronzed with colour.

It's nature, it's coming.

People put their jumpers on,
Animals get ready to hibernate,
We know it's coming.

It blows down chimneys
And whistles down roads,
It shivers down spines,
But leaves its footprints under trees.
The signs are clear that it is coming.

It's coming,
Autumn is coming.

Rebecca Talbot (12)
Norwich High School for Girls

Anger

You well up inside me,
Growing stronger every second,
Frantically searching for a way to escape,
A way to roam free,
Who are you?

Soon you are bursting, tearing,
Hurtling across the room,
Like a lion, so close to its prey,
Causing me to say things I don't really mean,
Who are you?

You slam against the wall,
Shattering into millions of pieces,
Making fear penetrate through the air,
Like the wild waves breaking on the rocks,
Who are you?

You cause people to cry
And others to hate,
While your sharp-pointed daggers you throw,
Piercing the 'once was' still sky that I used to know,
Who are you?

Your sound is of something unpleasant,
Destroying all that lies in your wake,
You twist and turn and writhe and scream,
All consuming,
Who are you?

Lashing out with your claws of fate
Or stamping out all joy,
Whatever you're doing, wherever you are,
I still wonder,
Who are you?

Emily Farrow (12)
Norwich High School for Girls

The Golden Land

The sun rises on a land of old,
Once powerful as the sky,
But the glory of their rule is cold,
Their magic left to die.

'The land of majesty,' some said,
'The wonder of the ancient world,'
But they have not stepped the path they led,
Before their reign was unfurled.

Egypt! Land of mystery,
What now do you want to see?
Golden pharaohs 'neath the sun
Or your structures fading one by one?

Your country was once rich in trade,
Your jewels in unmarked chambers laid.
The monuments which stood tall and proud,
With beauty and greatness endowed.

But now the land is still and dead,
The pharaohs gone in style,
The kingdom has laid down its head,
'Neath the shadows of the Nile.

Alicia Grix (12)
Norwich High School for Girls

Peaceful Sunset

I look in your eyes with wonder.
I see a peaceful sunset
descending slowly to the horizon,
almost gone . . . but not yet.

Its colours streak across the sky,
fluffy clouds go floating by.
As it comes down from its throne on high.
Each time it is different, no one knows why.

You resemble the sun as it falls,
moving with dignity and grace,
casting shadows on the walls.
I observe the flawless, steady pace.

The moon gets ready to appear,
as end of day is drawing near.
Birds stop their joyful song of cheer
as the sky begins to clear.

Before it sets, I want to hold this sun,
fill my life with its rays;
feast on the beautiful perfection,
then brightly I'll glow the rest of my days.

As nearer to the Earth it descends,
closer to my life it wends.
Then I'm stuck by the feeling I get . . .
for in your eyes is a peaceful sunset.

Hanna-Li Roos (12)
Norwich High School for Girls

My Little Stream

When I go on holiday to my grandma's,
There is a little stream next to the house
And an evergreen, pine tree forest
Separates the little stream from the road,
Sometimes I go there when I'm lonely,
Sometimes I go there when I'm bored,
Sometimes I go there when I'm happy
And often I go there to have fun,
My little stream is a good friend
And a good amusement for children,
They wreck it, they throw twigs
And misplace the stepping stones,
They block up the tube from where the water runs,
When I go there the next day,
To see my faithful friend,
I cannot hear the trickling water
Or see my stone around the bend,
I search high, I search low,
I search the whole area,
But do I find my pretty stone?
No! They've taken it,
Then tears come to my eyes
And I trudge slowly home,
For I'll never see my pretty stone,
In the water with the flow,
Then the next day,
I return to my good friend
Clear out the tube,
Plop
And see my stone again.

Alanah Reynor (12)
Norwich High School for Girls

Dawn To Dusk

I see the sunrise every day,
From start of June to end of May;
The pink, the red, the yellow too,
All contrast with the radiant blue.

The ten o'clock sunshine dazzling bright,
The world revolves in its lovely light;
By twelve, the sun is beating down,
The people beneath it are turning brown.

By one o'clock it's still quite hot,
The sun is just a shining dot;
Hanging there up in the sky,
Miles below the birds all fly.

Four o'clock, it's cooling down,
My smiling face is now a frown;
The red-hot day has got to me,
I long to splash around in the sea.

Six o'clock, there's still the light,
The sun's still shining oh so bright;
By ten o'clock, it's almost dark,
There is no sweet song of the lark

And so the sun has set at night,
The only glow is from the street light;
So here I watch the young owls play,
From dusk 'til dawn on this beautiful day.

Victoria Brooks (12)
Norwich High School for Girls

Christmas Eve

Wintertime begins
Snowdrops falling in
Falling through my window
A cool drift of snow comes in gently

Carol singers sing
Soft as a feathered wing
Mince pies and mulled wine
Are sitting by the fireside

The baubles are on the tree
Glistening with glee
The box of chocolates is open
And the best ones have gone

Grandad's sitting down
And I'm going to town

To see the special lights
The greens, the reds, the colours

Magic time is here
It's special, *that* is clear
Jesus, it's Your birthday tomorrow
And I will sing

I love Christmas time
And that is no crime
I'm getting really hopeful
For that nice, big red truck

I'm sitting on Granny's knee
And what do I see?
Santa Claus himself
As I drift off to sleep

Ding-dong, ding-dong go the bells
Sing song, sing song go the carols.

Imogen Cox (12)
Norwich High School for Girls

At Midnight

Midnight falls, an owl hoots in the distance,
The inky sky hangs over the vast empty wilderness.
A misty moon hides behind a sinister cloud,
The eerie silence is broken by the wind weaving like a snake
between the trees.
The river was black like dried blood in the distance,
Wolves howl at the moon, then the thunder rumbles.
A low vibration in the earth and the lighting flicks through
the atmosphere.
Trees swayed as the wind howled and raged.
Once again the sky was lit up with a streak and flash of anger.
The river waters yelped as they were violently spun and
pushed around.
The thunder roared as if it owned the sky.
Trees moaned and creaked at the force of the wind.
The moon had vanished, rubbed out like in a picture
And the growling of the wolves, matched that of the thunder.
Then as quickly as it had begun, it ended.
The thunder let out one more weak roll and the lightning gave
A pathetic flash of light and it was over.
The wind stopped whistling and the trees grew still.
The moon appeared, graceful, bright and round.
The river shone in the distance, like crystal on a ring.
A fox padded across the grass and all was calm.

Laura Robertson (12)
Norwich High School for Girls

Space

Where is space?
Is it here? Is it there?
It's over here,
No, it's over there.

Space is all around us,
Way up high,
Right down low,
Nowhere does it not dwell.

The stars,
The sun
And the Earth,
There is no escape from the places in space.

Space is full of joyous light,
Space is full of defeating dark,
Places full of people and song,
Places full of nothing and sadness.

What is space made of?
It is not anything,
But everything,
All the worlds combined.

How do we find space?
It is not to be found,
But to be left alone,
Yet we are always searching.

Alex Lawrence (12)
Norwich High School for Girls

Special

The Bible says
That God made the flowers, the trees, the animals,
The moon and the stars.
The Bible also says,
That God made me.
I look at the flowers,
With vivid colours
And intricate patterns
And at the trees,
With golden, crisp leaves in autumn,
Like fires on sticks.
I see the animals,
Deer jumping high,
Fish darting, silver streaks in the river,
Squirrels flashing up tree trunks.
Then I look up at the moon,
Silver in the night sky,
With its craters making a smiling face,
Watching me.
I see the stars!
Brighter than polished gems,
Like flames and sparks on an endless velvet cloak,
So far away and so beautiful.
Then I look up at a mirror
And see me, limp hair,
Knobbly knees, hopeless at maths,
But I think of my family and their love for me
And of the things I have achieved
And smile, because I know, in my own little way,
That I am special.

Frances Pickworth (12)
Norwich High School for Girls

Perfect Day

You smell the fresh cold air,
You feel the wind through your hair,
Your cheeks are pink,
Your breath is cold.

The sun is rising in the east,
The birds gather for their morning feast,
Berries on the trees,
Crumbs on the table.

A perfect way to start the day,
If only we could stay here to play,
Alas, things to do!
Alas, places to be!

Harriet Saunders (13)
Norwich High School for Girls

Colour

A fiery ball of light,
Disappearing into the darkness of the night.
Fiery-orange and flaming-red,
Merging like skin that's cut and bled.

Colours of the sun bleeding in the sky,
An explosion of colour about to die,
A sea of fire flooding the night,
A candlelit flame burning bright.

A sunset of beige,
Grey the colour of rage?
The colour of black and white,
Doesn't seem quite right.

A world without green and blue
Is like a soul without you,
A world without green and blue
Is almost untrue.

Nikila Patil (12)
Norwich High School for Girls

Flying

I'm flying in the sky
I go up very high
From here I can see the birds fly
I look down below
I can't see my little toe
I look down and see the people so low
I can see the farmer about to sow
I have no idea what's going on
Whether it's war, happiness, sadness
And then I think about a song
And wonder what is going on down below
Where not everyone is so low
I think about everyone on the go -
Nurse Joy, Doctor Dee and Farmer Joe
I suddenly realise what to do
And come down from where the sky is so blue
As I come down a plane flies high
But as I get lower, I can smell apple pie
I'm back on the ground
Then I hear a shouting sound
It's my mum
Calling me to fill my tum.

Athena Mills-Vingoe (13)
Norwich High School for Girls

My Best Friend

My best friend's disabled,
If I were her, I don't know what I'd do,
If I wasn't able to move,
I don't know how I'd feel,
I'd want to know why God made me special
And what it would be like to be like everyone else,
I'd be frustrated,
I know that,
Not being able to express my feelings,
Or show the people who jeer at me,
That I am real,
I'd want to have the same opportunities as everyone else
And a chance to get somewhere in life,
A target to set my sights on
And if I had one wish, I'd want to move again,
Just for one day to feel what it was like,
I'd want to scream at people for not letting me try things for myself,
Most of all I'd hate the guy who ran me over
And took away my chances and especially my life,
But my best friend keeps on going
And she lives life day by day,
But one thing's for sure,
She'll always be my best friend.

Alanna Cockburn (12)
Norwich High School for Girls

Away It Ran

Away it ran
Through the grey mist
Curiously I followed
Away it ran
Into the uninviting darkness
Cobwebs, jewelled with morning dew
Hung from it like earrings
Like millions of glittering studs
Glistening in the red morning sunlight
Away it ran
Under the tall shadowing trees
Bent into an arch
Away it ran
Crisp leaves crunching underfoot
It moved almost silently under the red sky
Away it ran
Until it reached the end of the forest
To the green fields where it stopped with a jolt
It had taken me home.

Louisa Kelf (12)
Norwich High School for Girls

The Swan

The sky is greying,
It will rain today,
The water ripples,
She lands.
Her snow-white colour,
Showing innocence.
The curve of her neck
Is grace,
Her gentle wings
Freedom,
She is hope.

Claire Mudge (12)
Norwich High School for Girls

The Sun

Golden yellow,
Shining brightly,
Burning, twirling,
Powerful, mighty,
Day to day,
Always bright,
Until the sky
Turns into night.

Fire so hot,
Years away,
Travels through space,
To make a day,
Planets twirl
And spin around,
In the silence of space,
It makes no sound.

Years and years,
It's shone so bright,
Years and years,
It's made the light,
Until it's burnt
Down to its core,
The sun will shine,
For evermore.

Temaloh Tempest-Roe (12)
Norwich High School for Girls

The Moon

It's a big ball of cheese,
Crusty, yellowish cheese,
Floating high up in the sky,
Levitating with ease!

It hides in the daytime
And comes out early eve
And lights up the night's sky,
Until it has to leave!

Neil Armstrong first touched . . .
The surface of the moon,
In nineteen sixty-nine
And others followed soon!

It is home to a man,
The man who's in the moon,
Who spends his days way up high,
Humming a dreamy tune!

We all see it at night,
Among the shining stars,
Far, far away from us,
But not as far as Mars!

Without it, nights would be dark,
Only stars up in the sky,
It's a part of our world,
You have to ask yourself, why?

Harriet Bryce (12)
Norwich High School for Girls

Swimming

We have swimming on Fridays
So we race to the school pool
Get changed and showered quickly
But don't run - that's a rule

We sit down on the pool edge
Dip toe tips in a dash
The teacher enters, eyes all strict
Making sure we don't splash

And then we do the warm-up
Four widths of fast frontcrawl
I clamber out exhausted
And lean wearily on the wall

But that was just a warm-up
There's much larger things to come
So we jog down to the deep end
(Not, of course, at a run)

Everyone dives smoothly
But I bellyflop - ow!
Then I plunge down a whole two metres
The depth the deep end will allow

I feel smooth and streamlined
Arms forward, legs blurring
Then I surface, gulping air
And my arms start quickly whirling

I'm sure I've got the stroke all wrong
As I reach the other side
But I really love the feeling
Of taking water for a ride.

Lucy Edwards (11)
Norwich High School for Girls

A Poem About A Poem

I was told to write a poem but I'd rather give it a miss,
I can't think of what to do, 'Please do my homework, Sis.'
If only I could think up a start,
I really wish I were that smart.
I just can't think of ideas for a subject,
Please Mum, 'Darling, you know I object.'
Should my poem be rhyme?
But no, I don't really have the time.

What language should I use?
Maybe similes, but not, I refuse.
They're as complicated as a spider's web,
Or as water swirls before the ebb.
I should use a metaphor of a kind,
But *splash* the thought is lost deep in my mind.

This poem is going all wrong,
I hear it and then I long,
That it wasn't due for tomorrow,
But this thought only brings sorrow.
Now I'm really for it,
I'll have to listen and sit
And watch everyone reading their part.
Why, oh why couldn't I make a start?

The taste of bitter on my tongue,
Reminds me the lesson has begun.
My mind is as blank as the clean white board,
The idea that flickered has gone, oh Lord!
Then what I've written I read,
Maybe this might fulfil my need.
My mind unravels from the caterpillar to the butterfly,
This will do, I grin and sigh.

Amelia Duncanson (14)
Norwich High School for Girls

Feeling Thoughts

Gorleston,
Gorleston-On-Sea.

The yellow glorious sand,
Walking through the sand,
Sounds like snakes slithering,
Covering land.

The blue crashing waves,
Dark blue waves crashing loudly,
As if horses were galloping in a hurry,
I always gaze at it.

I look and look,
My eyes,
Seem to be magnetised to the ocean
And glue is connecting
My feet to the ground,
As if my feet and the ground
Were pages sealed tightly of a book.

Standing there gazing at the sea!
I can't move and neither can my eyes . . .

Naveen Rizvi (11)
Norwich High School for Girls

Autumn

The leaves are falling all around,
Crushing, crashing and crunching to the ground,
Orange, brown, yellow and red
Are the colours to be found.

Fresh tastes of berries and apples,
Just recently picked,
After eating the warm pies
Our lips are licked.

Then outside we run to play in the snow,
We play every year - no matter how much we grow.

Snowman or snowball,
There's fun to be had for all.

After a day full of fun,
Inside to be we run.

A hot drink, served with cream,
Then off to bed for a sweet dream.

Jo Kalinowska (13)
Norwich High School for Girls

Nonsense Poem - Feelings

I face the sun, but I see the moon
And the moon looks back at me.
The stars on my face,
See the sun at rise.

I see snow,
But I feel sand.
I see blue sky,
But I feel rain.
Am I going insane?

Fiona Barrie (12)
Norwich High School for Girls

The Bervie Chipper

As I sat and stared out the window,
The droning voice of Mrs Bimbo
Washed over me as though I were dead,
Oh how I wished to be snug in my bed.

I felt the taste of Friday coming,
Whilst I sat there softly humming,
The greasy batter and salty chips,
I wasn't interested in science tips.

Every Friday after school,
We'd dash to the car and drive like fools,
So we could be the first out of the drive,
To the Bervie Chipper for half-past five.

The shiny tables, the polished floor,
Waiting for food as outside the rain poured
And finally it would arrive,
Golden, gorgeous, greasy, I picked up my knife.

Charlotte Coulthard (13)
Norwich High School for Girls

When Things Go Wrong

When things go wrong,
As they usually will
And life has hit the ground,
Your toast is burnt,
Your shoes don't fit
And nothing can be found.

There's a special someone,
To help you through these times,
A helping hand, a golden heart,
She's called your best friend.

Hannah Fraser (12)
Norwich High School for Girls

Yellow Flowers

He's shouting at us both but we don't hear him
All we know is that he's threatening us
We can't escape, we're trapped
In this car with him
Doing 60mph

Traffic lights - we're saved!
I grab her hand
I whisper -
He hears but I don't care
I wrench open the car door
She falls and I pull her towards me
We run . . .

We stumble and look behind
He's left the black prison at the lights, the BMW
He's following - people are yelling
We can't go any faster
She's too old for me to carry, even piggy style
No time to think
Can't stop - not now
I've gone too far
He's going to kill us both
I'm only 12; she's only 5 . . .
And we're going to die

I let her go, I betrayed her . . .
She'll die and I won't
But inside I'm dying of guilt - it's terrible
Shouting, petrol, mud, blood, sweat and tears remind me
I die all over again . . .
Yellow flowers.

Camille Chart (13)
Norwich High School for Girls

To Be Me

There's me in myself,
I pretend to be someone else,
Every time that small voice tells me my heart is thudding,
It is sad, I do not show it,
I can't help it,
'Yes you can.'
'No I can't, it's who I am:
Loud, scared, pressurised . . .'
There I go again,
A mad whirl of colour that is the world comes into focus.
I am prancing around and pretending this is me.
'It's not, I am you.'
That lovely voice is back again,
I listen to it as the world goes out of focus.
My fingers freeze in mid-air and my body tenses,
I am listening to it,
'Be yourself.'
'I am trying.'
'Not hard enough.'
'Don't push me.'
'You're pushing yourself . . .'
I relax and fall deep into my true being,
'This is you.'
The world starts up again,
I want to be me!
There's a smell caught under my nose,
Pencil shavings, school,
I'm back,
There's no turning back so I shall just go on pretending
To be me.

Jasmin Kirkbride (13)
Norwich High School for Girls

Harry

Harry was stuck in the bathroom,
The door was firmly locked,
Outside we sat and talked,
As Harry banged and knocked.

At first we just ignored him,
Drowsy from skiing all day,
We played cards and betted,
In the attic of the chalet.

Harry started shouting,
Chris said he'd help him out,
As he climbed out onto the roof,
I was filled with doubt.

I climbed out of the window,
To see if I could help Chris,
I could see the street down far below,
I nearly fell but he grabbed my wrist.

I was excited yet afraid,
A darkened silence hung in the air,
Chris took my hand,
We reached across and we were there.

We rescued Harry and climbed over the roof,
We tiptoed back as light as a feather,
I was terrified, it was scary,
But it was the best holiday ever!

Lucy Montagu (13)
Norwich High School for Girls

Cornwall

Sandy beaches; grassy cliffs
Brilliant sunshine; pouring rain

Last time I saw you - '99
Many summers have flown past
No more laughter in the sun
The fun times did not last

But the memories of Trevelgue
They always will remain
Memories of the golden sands
And of Cornwall's wind and rain

Long and sunny bike rides
The boat trips out to sea
Playing on the wooden beams
Where I fell and grazed my knee

One trip to the beach will remain in my mind
The five hours in the rain
You and I, your dad and mine
Sand-model building was our game

We shaped and formed our woman
Wind whipping sand into our eyes
Battling with the cold, hard rain
From bleak and dismal skies

But don't forget the good days
Of hot weather and lots of sun
Diving into the foaming sea
And, best of all, having fun!

Ellen Wasden (13)
Norwich High School for Girls

Autumn

As nights pull in and evening light fades
The leaves on the trees are all pretty shades
Of vermilion-red, burnt-orange and sunset-yellow
That tell the story of an autumn so mellow

The mornings are misty, cold and damp
Dewdrops on cobwebs shine like small lamps
The smell on the air of bonfires burning
That have smouldered all night with their embers glowing

Hedgerows heave with the dark juicy fruit
Of elder and blackberries for the birds to loot
Apples drop from the orchard trees, *plop*
How I wish autumn would never stop.

Gemma Johnson (13)
Norwich High School for Girls

A Memory

Along the motley river bank,
With shades of green and blue,
The modulating water flows,
A sound that I once knew.

The willow arched its August head,
Not a teardrop in its eye,
The birds and beasts amble free,
On land and in the sky.

Lilies like crowns of beauty,
Amongst the aquatic head,
A surge of cascading waters,
All a memory in my head.

Elizabeth Howard (13)
Norwich High School for Girls

I Stand Alone

Here I am, I stand alone
Within the wilderness
I stand boldly, my colour shining
Out for the world to see

Some crave me, while others see me for their own delight
But still I stand, quite alone
My face the colour of suffering, the suffering of so many
Many of those innocent
Others gone
Or so they say
Some are lost, but their spirits live on
Through my radiant petals

And still I stand
My own being as well as many others
I, the bare, forgotten
Poppy.

Rachel James (13)
Norwich High School for Girls

The Memories

My first little pony, brown and fluffy,
Reminded me of a teddy bear,
All round and scruffy.

His bright brown eyes and tiny feet,
Reminded me of a foal,
Frolicking to the beat.

His soft glossy tail touching the ground,
Reminded me of a feather boa,
Wrapped round and round.

Many years later, fluffy but old,
Reminded me of a grey badger,
Curled in the shelter, out of the cold.

Samantha Parker (13)
Norwich High School for Girls

A Fading Pawprint

The times we played amongst the green trees
Like sisters, we put each other's feelings at ease.
She had a voice only I could understand,
Stood by my side and made me so proud -
That I had the warm hearted one -

The one that would always come
When I needed her at desperate times.
The one that I could trust, the one that was kind.
She was my life, my soul, my heart,
How will I live now we've been driven apart?
Her silky ears that she hated me to touch,
Or her belly to be tickled, uh - then she wasn't so tough!
I'd talk to her strolling down the street,
Not caring what people may think or say,
On the grassy hills with the horses we would play.
I forget the times we would fight on the kitchen floor,
Of course she would win when I had to face those massive paws.
Though we'd always make up and cuddle yet again
And confide in each other's care.
But now she has moved to another carer,
My Rottweiler, my dog, my best bud:
My Tara.

Nikki Shattock (13)
Norwich High School for Girls

Hallowe'en

A house held by the night
All colours flee as black suffocates
This place
Led like martyrs
Into the darkness
That tries to conceal the corruption
Caught in the twilight that successfully
Steals our sight, so hands must see
Taken to the room where
The stagnant, stale air
Hangs around her body, waiting
For her to live so it may too
Her screams survive
So all may hear
The fear
From that night revived
As betrayed by her husband
The colour red braves the dark and she falls
We run, our mouth filled with a bitter liquor
The terror and adrenaline in this house entwined
Much like the cobwebs around your face
As you plunge through the corridors with haste
Driven by some sinister excitement
You try to run further, from your memory
From all your senses of what is seen
But you are safe in the knowledge that it's Hallowe'en.

Chloe Mashiter (13)
Norwich High School for Girls

Sweet Sensations!

It lay there in my hand,
A gold, shimmering wrapper with
Purple swirling writing.

Pulling the tabs at either end caused,
A heavy, hard, honey-coloured ball to
Roll into my hand.
The round shape was cold, smooth and hard.

I popped it in my mouth.

My tongue tingled as the pellet grew warm
And burst a buttery feeling
Everywhere inside my mouth.
Too hard to chomp and chew,
Yet far too tempting to let it lie there,
Slowly fading away.

I gingerly turned the toffee over
And started nibbling at the edge.
Chewing. Chewing.

A creamy chocolate taste flowed like a running stream
And mingled with the caramel.
Yummy!
I chewed faster and more furiously and . . .

It was gone.
The taste faded, my eyes sad, my mouth hollow.

It lay there in my hand,
A gold, shimmering wrapper with
Purple swirling writing.

Brigette Atkins (14)
Norwich High School for Girls

Far Away

Sometimes I lie in the sun,
dreaming about old and new.
Slowly the clouds roll past,
a never-ending patchwork of blue and white.
A pile of books is by my side
and as I lie there, my thoughts drift to them:
Oblivious to all, except the figures I see;

Warriors drawing their swords,
schoolgirls playing tricks on their teachers.
A quest for a stolen prize;
a battle for good or evil.
I live all their lives and find myself
crying when they are in pain or despair.
I feel their love and their hope.
I will never believe that they are just stories.
Their lives will be in my mind for as long as I live
and when I die I will join them.

Someone calls and I am back to being just me,
Reluctantly.

Camilla Mondon (13)
Norwich High School for Girls

Not Myself

Look up to her,
Want to be like her,
Hair as yellow as corn,
Skin like a baby born.

I am obsessed with her,
Everything about her!
Watch her play sport,
No body part contort.

Why am I so obsessed?
I feel like I'm possessed,
I'm not sure I want to be her,
I shouldn't be like this.

My obsession went too far,
It is over!
I am my own individual self,
I am no one but me!

Chloe France (11)
Norwich High School for Girls

The Race

My fingers pierce the surface,
Like a needle through silk.
I glide, glide,
Like a fish in the sea.

The waves cascading around me,
Like towering cliff tops,
All alone,
Easily propelling myself through the water.

My heart thumping,
Legs pumping!
Until . . .
It's over!

Harriet Easton (11)
Norwich High School for Girls

Friends Forever

If friends were pretty flowers
Growing strong and tall
I'd pick you out from all the rest
I'd never let you fall

I will always be there for you
No matter what you do
The playing and the laughing
Together, just me and you

Friends are like the shining sun
Gleaming up above
They are like a precious diamond
Which everybody loves

Friends are like the twinkling stars
Hanging in the sky
They are special and they're caring
Don't forget as time goes by

But at the end of the day
We will be together
So remember that we are
Friends forever!

Ozzy Gorman (12)
Norwich High School for Girls

My Emotions

When I feel cheerful,
There's a smile on my face,
I'm bright, breezy, bubbly,
The world is full of light.

When I feel sad,
There are tears in my eyes,
I'm doleful, downhearted, dispirited,
The world has gone all dark.

When I feel lonely,
I seem so far away,
I'm friendless, forlorn, forsaken,
The world is covered in mist.

When I feel angry,
I start to stamp and shout,
I'm irritated, indignant, incensed,
The world has gone all red.

Rachel Moxon (10)
Norwich High School for Girls

Happisburgh

S plashing waves lapping against the groins,
E ndless golden sands gritty to touch.
A ll is quiet as a mouse,
S till as a rock.
I nnocent seagulls squawking,
D iving into the salt smelling ocean,
E very boat bobbing out far in front of me.

D inky dolls are people,
A qua erodes the cliffs into the sea,
Y ellow glow falls on the water,
S unny happy seaside days!

Harriet Mark (12)
Norwich High School for Girls

Friendship

Friendship is like your favourite toy
Always there to comfort you in times of need
It may have tiny holes
Stitched up with brightly coloured embroidery thread

Friendship is evergreen
It is watered before it eventually grows
And creates the fine strong substance
That will always be with you

Friendship is more precious than the rarest gems
It cannot be bought for it is priceless
Yet it forms in contentment
Like the last piece in a jigsaw puzzle

Friendship can brighten up the darkest of days
Part the cloudy skies to reveal a watery sun
Like a piece of hope among the monsters of the river
Wherever you are it gives you faith and boosts your confidence

A world without friendship is a desolate place
A world without soul and meaning
Like a barren desert frozen in time
The world without friendship is empty and dry.

Freya Hocking (11)
Norwich High School for Girls

Friendship

You're my best friend, Jo,
You're really go, go, go,
You cheer me up at anytime
And you nearly read my mind!

You sometimes finish
My sentences for me,
I like your sense of humour,
Giggling with glee!

I like your sense of style,
You really make me smile,
You're really quite clever
And you're as light as a feather!

I like your funny jokes,
They cheer up lots of folks,
I like going shopping,
Jo, you're really quite hopping!

Hannah Rhodes (11)
Norwich High School for Girls

Imagine

I magine if there was no books to tell truth or tale,
M any lives would be wasted and many would all fail.
A nyone who tried to write these stories old or new,
G ave up after three attempts and always right on cue,
I ntently cried, 'I must have been deserted by the muse,'
N ever shall I forget to give a cow, on my weekly cruise
E ndurance is one thing, but that is just another,
If you had tried, you would have cried and that we shall not discover.

Hannah Moss (12)
Norwich High School for Girls

Love!

The sand felt smooth going between my toes,
The sea was gently lapping against the pebbles and stones,
Oh how I longed not to be alone,
But to have a partner of my very own!

When I first saw him, my heart skipped a beat,
He looked so sweet, good enough to eat!
He was the one, definitely for me,
Oh how romantic it was with the waves in the sea!

His dark brown eyes glistened in the light,
They sparkled like diamonds all day and all night!
He appeared to be handsome and looked so fine,
How I wanted him to be all mine!

I sat on a bench on my own you see . . .
When my Mr Right came and sat beside me,
We started to talk, you know how you do,
Looking at each other and smiling too!

We walked along the sandy beach,
Until the tide came into reach,
We said goodbye with a little kiss,
Now I had one and only wish!

My wish was that he would call me, as he had promised,
I think he will, for I think he was fairly honest,
The telephone rang, I jumped to my feet,
Once again my heart skipped a beat.

We went to dinner, it was divine,
He walked me home, our arms entwined,
We looked deep into each other's eyes
And then at once I knew he was
Mine!

Sophia Thompson (11)
Norwich High School for Girls

Joy Or Sadness

Eerie shadows fall over the land like thunder,
Thousands of crashes echo around like shooting stars,
Cloudy puffs of grey smoke condense by the second as death
Become nearer and nearer each time they breathe,
The wind whips by like a serpent,
Twirling and blowing on brave men's faces
Like a bullet surging through their bodies.
Fear flows through their minds as they force themselves
To fight through sheer determination.
Through sadness and the question,
Will I survive? As they take one more step and living or dying
To save the country's own power.
Sounds of guns firing and the sounds of planes circling in the mist,
Strikes of flowing fire light up the gloomy sky,
Drops of rain feel like cold blood from exhaustion,
Dodging and jumping into soggy trenches, out of reach
Of the dangerous daggers that shoot out of nowhere,
Ear-splitting sounds all around,
Thick, heavy smoke inhaled into men's lungs,
The concentration,
The determination,
The struggle,
Then there is none.
Scratches of brambles tear across their faces
Like a cat feasting its claws into its prey,
Squeezing every piece of energy out of each man
Until there is no longer the man that stands to fight.

Emma Slater (11)
Norwich High School for Girls

Feelings For My Puppy

Sometimes he makes me happy,
Sometimes he makes me mad,
I love my puppy very much,
But he can be so bad.

I cried the day he ate my toy
And ripped apart my book,
But he wagged his tail,
Then gave me his best look.

My life is fun now he is here,
He's full of bounce and joy,
I'd miss him so very much
If anyone took my boy.

My heart would break if he was ill,
I really couldn't cope,
Sandy is such a lovely dog
And fills me full of hope.

Hannah Barringer (11)
Norwich High School for Girls

The Journey

Water flows silently
Running down the stream
Winding down the mountain
Shining like diamonds in the sunlight
Singing to the birds and flowers along the way
Passing through the whispering trees
Carrying along the leaping fish
Rushing through the boulders
With the sound of thunder
Falling over the precipice
Into the glistening pool below.

Laura Thompson (11)
Norwich High School for Girls

Why War?

War is like a raging beast,
Prowling ever closer.
Through barren deserts and snow-capped mountains,
Bringing with it poverty and disease.

War is like a poison-filled dagger,
Threatening the world.
It does no good to anyone,
Even those whose wage it will suffer.

War is like a gaping black hole
That has spread its way through harmony,
Swallowing up peace and tranquillity,
With death, terror and panic put in their place.

War is like a vast shadowing cloud,
Which suddenly, with no warning, will spill out its evil.
Danger, destruction and devastation will enter
And there is no end in sight.

So, I ask you, why war?

Alice Prinsley (11)
Norwich High School for Girls

Black Is As Blue As Yellow

Black is as blue as yellow
And yellow is as blue as black
Mud is as clear as a glass palace
And the glass palace is as clear as mud
The stars shine black
Black shine the stars
The river flows still
Still flows the river
I'm facing forwards, walking backwards
I'm walking backwards as I face forwards
This poem is at the end but still at the beginning
This poem is still at the beginning but has come to an end.

Claire Palmer (13)
Norwich High School for Girls

The Tennis Game

Up, ping, swish, flick
Over it goes, skimming so quick
Dropping, dipping like a rocket
Right into its allotted socket

Back it comes just as fast
Gosh, she's hit – whoosh it's past
Here I go, serve again
Must be quick before the rain

We've changed the sides and she is serving
Here it comes, boy, it's curving
Oops, I lost that, now we're joint
This one will decide the point.

Yeah!

Katie Hewson (11)
Norwich High School for Girls

Shoes

I come in a long brown box,
I am black with rough edges,
I have a grey lace with split ends,
My rubber is scratchy,
My name is Mr Shoe,
I am a teacher
And teach all the young makes,
My wife is tall and slim,
With neat edges so fine,
She has a big black heel,
Her name is Mrs Shoe,
She teaches teenager makes,
Her favourite make is Nike,
But Kickers is a bit naughty.

Charlotte Kenny (11)
Norwich High School for Girls

Dad's Eccentric Hobby

Although I've never tried it,
My one desire in life,
Is to soar across the open sky,
With my children and my wife.

However I'm glued to the kitchen sink,
Or cleaning out the gutter,
But when I tell my hobby to the family,
They think I'm a nutter!

To spread my wings and catch the thermals,
Would be out of this world to me,
I'd glide over valleys, mountains and rivers,
Like a seagull over the sea.

But I must be happy and grateful,
For what I've already got,
Though I wouldn't mind trying hang-gliding,
I think I would like that a lot!

Katy Lines (12)
Norwich High School for Girls

Time

If the world one day,
Spins the opposite way,
Maybe time would change,
Times of monsters,
Times of magic.
Times when kings and queens had curses,
Times when Shakespeare wrote his verses.
Times when frogs turned into princes,
When kissed by a certain princess.
Times when people were beheaded,
Times when people would regret it if . . .
The world one day *did* spin the opposite way.

Isobel Crane (12)
Norwich High School for Girls

Goldfish

Goldfish, goldfish, now you're just an old fish,
It started off fine, it was a great idea,
A trip to the pet shop because goldfish aren't dear.
I chose the ones that looked the best,
I carried them home really close to my chest.
My very own pets to feed and to care,
A gleaming new bowl for them both to share,
The unfortunate thing was a lack of knowledge,
I might as well have filled the bowl with porridge!
The water was clean, not too hot, not too cold,
I lowered them in - a sight to behold!
But there are hidden things that cannot be seen,
A fish killing chemical - they call it chlorine.
They seemed to be happy enough for the first few hours,
Darting around in and out of the towers.
Now I was happy, my very own pet,
A cheap one too because they never need a vet!
I dreamt of them as I lay in my bed
But when I woke up, they were both dead.
An important lesson that needs to be learnt,
Dechlorinate your water or your fish will get burnt!

Marie Mallinder (12)
Norwich High School for Girls

Imagine

Imagine a world with no water,
a world so dry that the ground looks like a jigsaw with no pictures.

Imagine a garden with no flowers,
nothing to brighten the many sorrows in your day.

Imagine a school with no children,
no sounds of laughter or paintings on the bare walls.

Imagine a sky with no stars,
just a black mass of never-ending darkness.

Imagine a world with no sun,
no plants, animals or anything that ever lived.

Imagine a world with no love,
never any happiness and nobody caring for life or death.

Imagine . . .

Lucy Craig (11)
Norwich High School for Girls

My Friend

I've known my friend since I was born,
We go to the park together,
We go to each other's home and play,
She just lives next door,
We play jokes on everyone,
From putting pepper in people's drinks,
To putting glue on people's chairs,
When we play football and we smash a window
And we get in trouble, we get punished together,
Neither of us stands by ourselves,
Now the day's at an end and it's time to go home,
But we stop by the door, we thought,
No, let's play a trick on next-door's cat!

Gemma Lam (11)
Norwich High School for Girls

Why?

Why did I come to this cold and lonely room?
People coughing all over your face,
As if you haven't got enough to worry about,
Then they call your name,
Your heart beats faster and faster,
As you walk to the door saying, 'Yeah, I'm here.'

The lady in white says, 'He'll see you straight away.'
As if there's some kind of emergency
And that panics you even more.
She opens the door and you hear 'Take a seat.'
And he gets out your file.

He talks for a while about how not to worry,
How you will cope and he will be there if you want to talk,
Then you hear the words, 'More tests, to be sure.'
And you think to yourself, *why?*

If you knew how hard it was for me to come here today,
Then why put me through it again
Without telling me what the problem is?
Then I just ran out of the room
And think, *what is the meaning of life?*

Helen Auger (12)
Norwich High School for Girls

The End

The end separates good and bad,
You want to stay with Mum and Dad,
But time is running out,
If you want to stay in Heaven,
Not the other place, the bad place.

Nothing's wrong with the pure paradise,
With tinted rivers, cold as ice,
Smooth as glass, cleaner than white,
The sun burning bright,
Completing a warm spectacular sight.

Souls live in harmony,
Basking under fresh trees,
Regarding innocent squirrels,
with bottle-brush tails,
Listening to the sweet blue tit's song.

Though when you walk into blackness,
There's a burning desire to leave.
Look around the fiery canyons,
Littered with smouldering eyes,
Full of hatred, lust and loathing.

Hear screams of anguish,
Suffering under red-hot pokers,
Feeling fire under your skin,
Your feet scorched on the very floor,
Where grass is withered and dead.

The end separates good and bad,
You want to stay with Mum and Dad,
But time is running out,
If you want to stay in Heaven,
Not the other place, the bad place.

Georgia Levell (12)
Norwich High School for Girls

The Land Of The Free

I lay in my bed, a quiet place,
Away from the noise and rat race.
I lay there thinking and this came to me,
How lucky we are to live in a land that is free.

We have choices to make every day,
We know they will stay.
Little things, what to wear,
It's our way which's fair.

Some countries' choices are taken away,
Women are killed for wearing the wrong in the day.
I am lucky to live in the land of the free,
A kid is all I want to be.

We do have some rules, they are called the law,
It's not perfect, it has a flaw.
I believe in the law and what it stands for,
It's to protect us from harm, from starting a war.

I respect our fire brigade and police force,
For protection they are our source.
Putting their lives on the line every day,
To make sure we're OK,
From the evil that is out there today.

Bejal Godhania (12)
Norwich High School for Girls

Rubbish And Reminders

I'm tidying under my bed
Dust and fluff combined
Beads and bits of paper
A sticky sweet there too
A bashed up party popper
Some streamers and confetti

I'm sorting through the rubbish
A very tedious job
There's blue fluff and there's green fluff
A shrivelled up balloon
A piece of last week's homework
Hey, now that's where it has been

There are boxes and bags
Buttons and bows
Needles, threads and string
There are pictures and postcards
A drawing or two
A tissue and a bouncy ball

Memories and thoughts come flooding back
Friends and family, places I've been
Images return of loving times
I laugh at photos
And unbelievable things
Did that really happen? I thought it was a dream

Looking back is rewarding
But now you must always remember
And never forget
The very simple message
Don't look back to things which have gone
Only look forward to things yet to come.

Emily Smith (12)
Norwich High School for Girls

Who Talks?

For forty-one years I've waited,
In the dank dark dusty cellar,
I'll save it for a special occasion,
That's what he'd always said.

Now the occasion was special,
Here I am on the table,
His knife slits under my wax seal,
I'm uncorked, a classic vintage.

I'm poured into two slender glasses,
My bouquet is of summer's long forgotten
And distant fruits of childhood memory,
Let me breathe.

My liquor races ice and fire
To every nerve ending,
Sparkling memories,
Corroding the haze of time.

My job is done, my magic's worked,
I'm evaporating into familiar darkness
And here I'll stay till the end,
Wine talks, everyone knows that.

Frances Vincent (12)
Norwich High School for Girls

Up, Up And Up

Moving quickly through the air
Soaring high in the sky
Flying, flying, they aren't stopping
They move so swiftly without a sound

Journey ahead precarious
A scary one at that
Will they make it on time?
They help each other from day to day

Safety in numbers
Helps them on their way
What is the weather going to be like?
Helpful? Frightening or scary?
They have no idea of the adventure ahead.

Will lightning strike?
Will storms brew?
Will one die?
Will they have a fright?

Looking up at the sky,
I can feel the apprehension,
By their high pitch,
Shrilling noise that is blown down to me,
In the wind.

My voice is hardly audible now,
As I whisper good luck, goodbye!
The flock of birds fly away.

Lisa Carroll (13)
Norwich High School for Girls

Old Dog

Old dog
childhood friend
golden curls tumbling past
deep, mysterious eyes
like water in a well

Soft, gentle paws
wandering aimlessly around
the house
sleeping in the garden
lapping up the sunshine
like water

Eyebrows flecked with age
the inferno of youth
diminishing to a single flame
flickering in the darkness
the serrated claws of death
scratching mercilessly
at the old animal's heart
until one day
they pierce
and memories flood.

Imogen Calderwood (12)
Norwich High School for Girls

Leave Me

He opens the door,
Looks around,
He sees me crawling on the ground,
He swings me up and swings me in the air
And whispers softly in my ear,
Please do not leave me.

Five years now have gone by,
I sit here and cry,
Knowing I should have said the same,
Maybe he would still be here today,
Daddy, why did you leave me?

We had trouble in the past,
Life keeps on dropping bombs,
Since my daddy has gone,
That same question I've asked myself all my life,
'Why did you leave me?'

Gabriella Wells
Norwich High School for Girls

A Witch's Scream?

Screams, screams, screams in the snow,
Was she guilty? I don't know.

They ducked her in the duck pond,
She floated to the top,
They locked her in the dungeon,
The cruelty didn't stop.
They dragged her out in front of us,
Chains stilling her kicks,
Screams no one could listen to,
When fire met the sticks.

Screams, screams, screams in the spring,
Riding round the countryside, a ghostly, ghastly ring.

Jennifer Dell (12)
Norwich High School for Girls

Blue

Serenity as I look upon the turquoise fading light as the
sun goes down.
The royal horizon soon leaving like the sun ready to return
the next day.
The sky; a vast empty space of nothing just an atmosphere of nothing,
nothing, nothing.
As your pale eyes flicker past mine, I know we'll never see
each other again.
Forever goodbye, goodbye, goodbye, goodbye.
All good things come to an end and even the strongest friendships.
As the green sea laps up against the shore eroding at its path.
Water strike.
Another person dies as their water supply, their life source is
shattered and lacerated.
The world is made up of blue.
The world is empty without it.

Indea Cadman-Rivers (12)
Norwich High School for Girls

My Way To Build A Rainbow

My way to build a rainbow is to start off at the start,
Each and every meaning must come from in the heart.
You must start with the colours like toddlers' building blocks,
Red roses ripen as the love stands without a doubt,
Orange fires glaze in the longing winter nights,
While yellow is like happiness on a summer's sunny day,
Green glistening grass as the morning dew awakes,
Near the sky so blue by the lavishing country lakes,
Two purples come together by the vineyard with the grapes,
Finally, white and black stand for themselves and aren't
on the rainbow's list,
Next time you see a rainbow, think and make a wish.

Hannah Preston (12)
Norwich High School for Girls

True Life

As I make a new print on the frosty white ground,
My heart beats faster . . .
Nearer and nearer to school I get,
Around the corner and up Newham Road is all.
It's been a week since Nana's died.
I can feel a tear rolling down my cheek,
Why did she leave me?
I wipe away the tear with my icy cold hand,
Not wanting to give the bully and her foolish gang a chance.
That is all it would take, to push me off my cliff.
I have reached Newham Road, earlier than I thought.
My hands tremble with fear and dread.
My legs are giving way.
I can just imagine it . . .
Them staring at me as if I'm an alien from outer space.
Whispering and laughing at me.
Their stares boring into me as burning torches.
If only I had a single companion to comfort and support me,
I would pull through this dark, long, scary tunnel.
But how can they see me as me?
Not a big, gigantic, fat lump with no heart or feeling.
How can you blame them even if the teachers do the same thing?
Even timid Miss Hall absent-mindfully said, 'Pull your weight
around, Jo.'
Hope . . .
What and where is it?

I am so distant from it! It is over the horizon . . .
Somehow there will be a light to guide me through my
never-ending tunnel!
But when will that day be?

Divya Nelson (12)
Norwich High School for Girls

My Home

Water has turned to slime,
Ice cream is now spinach,
At least that's what it feels like
Since I moved far, far away.

Dollars have turned to pounds,
Sneakers are now trainers,
Candy has turned to sweets
And soccer is now football,
At least that's what it seems like
Since I moved far, far away.

I miss all my friends,
I miss the winter's snow,
The girls skating in parks,
The clapping to the President,
The schools with no uniform,
I miss it all.

Although I feel down
And England has weird words,
I love the fish and fries
And the little Norwich market,
Although I miss America,
I do like England too,
That fresh country air
And those home-made pies!

Jessica Allen (12)
Norwich High School for Girls

The Horse

The horse waits,
Wandering and tired,
The lids of its eyes,
Nearly touching.
Its stomach rumbling,
With no food to feed it.
Body barely twitching,
As it stands dead still.
It is patient,
But hot and bored,
Is any movement present?
I think that if it rained there now,
There would be a dry patch,
Showing the whiskers
And the fine fur,
Dry on the bare grass.

Virginia Fellows (11)
Norwich High School for Girls

The Bus

We drive to the bus stop at a quarter past seven,
Hoping the bus won't arrive at half-past eleven.

There I am standing in the freezing cold,
The bus is always late, so I've been told.

Alas, the rumours are true; it arrived at a quarter to eight,
Now I'm going to miss assembly because it's so late.

Squashed flies on the windows and gum on the floor,
Sometimes I think *I can't take anymore.*

Occasionally fast most of the time slow,
How annoying when we've got places to go.

Finally I arrive at Norwich Girls' High,
It's a shame that humans aren't able to fly.

Becky Powell (12)
Norwich High School for Girls

Best Friend

Everybody needs a best friend,
Someone to be there,
Someone to care.

Everybody needs a best friend,
Someone to hold our hand,
Someone to understand.

Everybody needs a best friend,
Someone to bring us through,
Someone to love you.

Everybody needs a best friend,
Someone to walk nearby,
Someone to never lie.

But there's none much better than can be,
A man's best friend, a small puppy.

Laura Bamford (11)
Norwich High School for Girls

Autumn Days

Weather changing, cooler days
Darker earlier, less time to play
Rusty-brown leaves falling on the ground
Making a small and colourful neat mound
The freshly ploughed fields sprouting greens
Cut by massive combine machines

Blackberries fill the country lanes
Swollen by the summer rains
Orchards full of crunchy apples
Just in time to decorate churches and chapels
For as we celebrate another harvest time
We say goodbye to summer and this rhyme.

Hannah Greeves (11)
Norwich High School for Girls

Excuses

As I was coming to school, Sir,
To do my experiments,
A car ran over me, Sir
And then a 4x4,
They took me to the hospital, Sir
And they said I'd be OK.

It's a shame it squashed my school bag
And my homework flew away,
It was only maths, RE and science, Sir,
I'm sure that's OK.

Why are you going red in the face, Sir?
Are you going to sneeze?
Here's a tissue just in case, Sir,
Are you feeling OK?
You look a bit bleary-eyed, Sir.

Can I go to lessons, Sir?
Oh, by the way, I lost Mum's letter
To say I can't do PE, Sir.
I lost it when I was run over, Sir,
Do I still do PE, Sir?

Emma Cooper (12)
Norwich High School for Girls

Sadness

I think I'm dying
For my petals are falling
And my leaves are rotting
I'm no longer thirsty
My strength is fading
I'm full of woe

I think back to when
My stem was straight
And my petals were turquoise-blue
My leaves were shining
I was thirsty then
But now I'm full of woe

Who is this here?
They're taking a flower
Which is going to be pressed
So I'll be preserved
Forever and ever
So not now am I full of woe.

Charlotte Pooley (11)
Norwich High School for Girls

Holiday

Waves crash,
I dash
Out of the raging sea.

Waves roll,
I stroll
Along the sandy beach.

Gulls screech,
I reach
For my mint ice cream.

Gulls bob,
I sob,
I've dropped my mint ice cream.

Boats hoot,
I scoot
Down to see them in.

Boats glide,
I hide
And watch the sun go down.

Stars twinkle,
I sprinkle
Sand into the sea.

Stars wink,
I sink
Down into my bed.

Elizabeth Fisher (11)
Norwich High School for Girls

I Can't Write Poems, Miss!

I can't write poems, Miss, I don't know what to say,
Whenever I try to start one, it goes wrong in every way.

I really can't write poems, Miss, I don't know what to put next,
Anything I do think of, is completely far-fetched.

I seriously can't write poems, Miss, it makes me feel quite wheezy,
Actually even Sarah can do it, it's got to be easy.

I *can* write poems, Miss, I know just what to say,
Whenever I start one, it goes right in every way.

I really *can* write poems, Miss, I know exactly what to put next,
Anything I think of, I can assure you is the best.

I seriously can write poems, Miss, I think I'm better than you are,
I'm sooooo brilliant, I could even be a poem-writing star.

I definitely can write poems, Miss, 'I know, you've been driving me round the bend.'
Ah-oh there's just one problem, I don't know how to end!

Sophie Dowson (11)
Norwich High School for Girls

I Used To . . .

I used to be so young and fit,
I even won sports day, I mean, can you believe it?

My legs were strong and good at sprinting,
'You'll be in the Olympics soon,' my friends kept hinting.

I would run around all day long
And when my shoes came off . . . oh Lord what a pong!

I used to walk to school each morning
And then back again as the day was drawing.

I was even in the football team
And when we won, Mum's face would gleam.

But now I'm old and I just drink tea,
No one would ever believe that that was me!

Millie Hepworth (11)
Norwich High School for Girls

My Little Sister

My little sister has accidents on the floor,
My little sister dribbles on the door,
She pulled Floppie's leg off,
She even crawled on my favourite cloth.

At nursery she makes a mess,
But all the teachers just say bless,
She'll always eat the Lego that's blue,
Her invisible friend, Anna, is just as bad too!

At the table she flicks food,
She'll call my brother *cool dude*,
But will she call me Jude?
No, she'll call me Gertrude!

At school she'll write upside down
And she'll call me a big fat clown,
She carved her name on my favourite tree
And she threw her rubber at me!

I think she really is just fine,
She just steps her foot one out of line,
Even though she is a bit . . . weird,
I suppose I'll be able to live with it.

Sophie Martin (11)
Norwich High School for Girls

If My Family Were Animals

If my mum was an animal,
She would be a horse,
Because horse's can be strong and forceful,
But kind and gentle too.

If my dad was an animal,
He would be a polar bear,
Because polar bears can be fierce
And also warm and fluffy through and through.

If my sister was an animal,
She would be a monkey,
Because monkeys can be naughty or nice,
But very cheeky too!

If my little sister was an animal,
She would be a fluffy mouse
Because mice are small and cuddly
And as sweet as can be.

If I was an animal,
I would be a dolphin,
Because dolphins are friendly
And fun to be with.

Laura Palmer (11)
Norwich High School for Girls

Why?

The ocean's a waste ground,
The sea is not blue,
What will there be
For me or for you?

The air is not clear,
For the chimneys are tall,
The hole in the ozone,
Is no longer small.

The rainforest is dying,
Through man's utter greed,
So why don't we stop?
The world is in need.

The landscapes are wide,
All covered in waste,
With rubbish piled high,
To nobody's taste.

Man is so greedy,
You hear the Earth sigh,
For if we don't stop,
The world would just die.

We must now all appreciate
And keep our world fair,
For greed's not the answer,
We must all try to care.

Alexandra Beatty (11)
Norwich High School for Girls

My Brother

My brother is sooo annoying
He always gets me into trouble
And when we fight like brothers and sisters do
Who gets the blame? The oldest, so in other words *me!*

My brother, he always winds me up,
He pulls rude faces at me so I pull them back,
But when I do, he tells on me and guess what happens?
I get told off.

My brother makes you want to give him a piece of your mind
But then he can be friendly and it makes you quite worried
But that's when the trouble starts.

My brother and me always fight, especially about whose
Programme is next and who's in the front on the way to school,
But my brother is 6 years old but acts like he's 2.

But together he's not too bad,
I really do love him, but only sometimes,
I just can't wait until he is 16 when he will probably be stronger
Than me, so I should watch out because it will be payback time!

Francesca Goodwins (11)
Norwich High School for Girls

Night

Night is the time of witching hour
Night is the time monsters lurk under your bed
Night is a fright for most people

Night is silvery
Night is cold
Night is very, very bold

Night is as dark as a sack
Night is as eerie and spooky as a ghost
Night! The stars are as sparkly as silver glitter

Night is silvery
Night is cold
Night is very, very bold

Night is silvery-white
Night smells of delight
Night is the time when days come to an end

Night is silvery
Night is cold
Night is very, very bold

As I walk through the woods
I find out things about the night
I see loads of things

Night is silvery
Night is cold
Night is very, very bold

I find white shadows which are ghosts
I find monsters behind the trees
I screamed and ran for my life!

Night is silvery
Night is cold
Night is very, very bold!

Charlotte MacIver (11)
Norwich High School for Girls

The Grandfather Clock

The grandfather clock stood stiff in the hall,
It waited and watched over us all
And listened to all our worries and strife
And it kept tick-tocking 'til the end of its life.

The grandfather clock stood proud and high,
Pendulum swinging as the hours went by,
It was beautifully inlaid with gold,
It still had many stories to be told.

The grandfather clock was decades old,
We haven't much money; it would have been sold,
Through the generations it has been passed down,
Its colour has changed to an orangey-brown.

But the house is still and cold,
On the clock is a layer of mould,
Much to our disappointment and woe,
Our clock stopped ticking many years ago.

Sanchia Rodrigues (11)
Norwich High School for Girls

Flight

An endless journey into space
Going at a super pace.

Bumblebees buzzing by,
In search of nectar for the hive.

A bird soaring through the sky,
Zooming down to catch a fly.

A frisbee whizzing through the air,
Quickly catch it over there.

A dragonfly with wings of blue,
Hovers over our pond and views,

An aeroplane with whirring blades,
Filled with children, buckets and spades.

What do I see? A bright pink kite,
Swooping around to children's delight!

Moths flying around by the moonlight,
Although it is the middle of the night.

A heron gliding over the broad,
Watch it swoop and soar.

A hot air balloon drifts slowly by,
Until the wind decides to die.

Millie Rhead (11)
Norwich High School for Girls

A New World

(Inspired by 'His Dark Materials Trilogy' by Philip Pullman)

I lie in my bed and rest, with the Northern Lights upon my chest
And as I read, I look through the eyes of Lyra staring up to the skies,
The things she sees, the coloured lights, shimmering, shining
soft and bright,
But most of all the world in the sky, so real, so clear, so
far away, so high.

I blink, I am back in my room, the lights have vanished, all that's
left is the moon,
It shines at me through my window, I turn away to face my pillow,
I stare at my book and as I do, the Northern Lights become real too,
The spine splits, light shines through, a dazzling shade of
electric-blue,
With the blue comes a vibrant red, it fills my room like water and
ripples round my head.

Every single colour continues to flood through, until my room is
filled with a beautiful rainbow,
But then the colours cease and out of them emerges a world
the colour of peace.

As I stare the lights come back, they form a bridge strong
and compact,
I start to climb and after some time,
I find myself in snow and ice, but to me it's paradise.

The world where I've always longed to go, and here I am
standing in its snow,
The cold is harshly biting in, the miles of frost are glistening,
I look down at my hands and am surprised to find, tough mittens
strapped to them warming and kind.

And then I realise I'm in reindeer furs, suddenly I hear soft
distinctive purrs,
I reach gently into my pocket, and find an ermine nestling into it,
My furs smelling of leather and wet dog, have kept it warm through
the snowy fog.

And then my thoughts creep back to my book, doesn't all this have
a familiar look,
I carefully, gingerly feel around and soon what I'm looking for
I have found,

The alethiometer in its oil skin pouch, wrapped in velvet, I
open my mouth.
Now I have no doubt who we are, me and Pan my second half,
I am Lyra Silvertongue, and my deamon Pantalaimon,
We look upon the amazing bridge and to the world beyond, from
whence I once came, but do not now belong
And as I cross I know I will not go back to my room, but to where
Lyra went after Roger's doom.

Phoebe Young (12)
Norwich High School for Girls

Deep Below

The cold water ripples as she swims underneath,
She dives down deeper as daylight comes,
The swish of her tail when she can hear a sound,
Her big, lonely eyes looking around.

Her green scaly skin shines in the moonlight,
As her flippers pull her down deeper, deeper,
She glides and slides through the water,
Like a feather through air.

Her breathing's so heavy yet she's not out of breath,
She calls for a friend but hears no reply,
Slowly, slowly she sinks down,
To the deep dark depths below.

She has been here waiting for thousands of years,
Yet no one knows she is real,
As she waits and waits for a long lost friend,
But I think she knows she has no one to wait for.

For she is all alone in the world.

Nicole Ross (11)
Norwich High School for Girls

Collector

(Based on 'The Sound Collector' by Roger McGough)

The sound collector came this morning,
In his black suit and tie of grey,
Caught every sound that he could find
And took them all away.

The frying of the bacon,
The sizzling of the egg,
The wailing of the baby,
When it's time to go to bed.

The whirring of the tumble dryer,
The banging of a door,
The rushing water from the tap,
He just grabbed more and more.

The squawking of the birds,
The whisper of the breeze,
The hissing of the grass,
As it rustles round your knees.

There's nothing left to hear
And not much left to see,
But how that stranger stuffed it all in his briefcase,
Is the mystery to me.

Priya Crosby (11)
Norwich High School for Girls

Ingredients

Magic touch, magic smell
Magic taste, magic spell

A pinch of evil to make the skin itch
A slurp of love to make the heart glitch

Magic touch, magic smell
Magic taste, magic spell

A fan of feathers from a phoenix tail
A gurgle of waves upon which ships sail

Magic touch, magic smell
Magic taste, magic spell

A choking fume from a wreaking skunk
A mild dose of heavy metal red-haired punk

Magic touch, magic smell
Magic taste, magic spell

Half a millimetre of the blackest death
A second helping of sly, sneaky theft

Magic touch, magic smell
Magic taste, magic spell

And this is the curse to make your eyes sting
And the Devil to leap on your back
But forever and ever the wind will whistle
Fear as an emotion is essential
That's magic!

Angharad Everden (11)
Norwich High School for Girls

The Rain Dancers

To the sound of the drums
Here it comes
To the sound of the drums it comes

To the sound of the feet
To the feel of the beat
To the sound of the feet it comes

To the cloth so bright
Like a spark in the night
To the cloth so bright it comes

To the colourful bangles
To the jings and the jangles
To the colourful bangles it comes

To the long beaded sticks
To the chants and the clicks
To the long beaded sticks it comes

To the parched grassland
To the dust and the sand
To the parched grassland it comes

As the magic is spoken
The great heavens open
And they dance to the sound of the rain.

Virginia Sorensen-Pound (12)
Norwich High School for Girls

I Take You For Granted

I know a person,
She's very special to me,
I take her for granted sometimes,
But she's very special to me.

We laugh together, cry together,
Giggle together, shout together,
We do everything together (more or less),
That's what makes her special.

When I need help, she's there,
When I need comfort, she's there,
When I need cheering up, she's there,
When I need her most, she's there.

I sometimes take this for granted.

We fall out sometimes, it's normal,
But we always come together again, that's the point,
I wouldn't give her up for a million pounds,
I wouldn't give her up for the world.

I can't lose her now,
We know each other too well.

We eat lunch together,
We joke together, that's the magic of it,
It all seems unreal but she's there, I know,
The most special girl I know.

Have you guessed it yet?
It's my friend, Faé!
I sometimes take her for granted,
It's amazing the magic she can do.

She's not a witch, a wizard or anything like that,
She's my friend and that alone is truly magical.

Lizzie Lloyd-Wickens (11)
Norwich High School for Girls

Christmas Magic

A joyful time is coming
It's full of fun and laughs

Is it the new year
With memories shining like beams of light
And fireworks exploding all through the night?
It's not the new year

A joyful time is coming
It's full of fun and laughs

Is it Easter
With crisp pancakes large and hot
Chocolate bunnies and eggs, why ever not?
It's not Easter

A joyful time is coming
It's full of fun and laughs

Is it Hallowe'en
With trick or treating
Ghosts, ghouls and pumpkin eating?
It's not Hallowe'en

A joyful time is coming
It's full of fun and laughs

Is it Christmas
With gifts and snow?
We are waiting for Santa
As he is too slow

It is Christmas.

Kirsty McRoberts (11)
Norwich High School for Girls

The Moon

I sit outside
Howling at the night
I look up at the sky
The silvery moon
Looks kindly down at me
Its solid, silvery shape
Lights up the whole night sky
Little stars puncture the never-ending night
The night gets darker and deeper
A blanket of cold wraps around me
I look around
In the dark nothingness

Clouds engulf the moon
Everything goes pitch-black
It's like nature's power cut
Now the night doesn't seem so safe
All the trees make dark shapes
Monstrous, evil shapes
Their boughs creak
As they lean over me
The cold makes my teeth chatter
My hair stands on end
All along my back
I hear footsteps behind me
I turn around
My mind is playing tricks on me
The moon becomes visible again
Its solid, silvery shape
I howl at the moon.

Victoria Lipp (11)
Norwich High School for Girls

Nobody

My life flashes before my eyes,
How boring it has been.
No one to love, no one to care,
Someone *must* have let me in.
I can't remember being helped,
Not in any way at all.
I helped lots of other people,
They just helped me fall.
Everybody hated me,
I did not hate them.
No one wanted to be my friend,
They had all their dens.
At school I was a loner,
At work I was one too.
I was questioned in my senior age,
For things I didn't do.
But now my life has ended,
I can sit back and relax.
Still living all on my own,
Not getting on people's backs.
If you are reading this poem
And you are without a friend,
Either go and try to make some,
Or like me, have a dismal end.

Sophie Baker (11)
Norwich High School for Girls

What Do I Do?

All I can hear is splash, splash, splash
I'm not meant to be here, I should be at home
I'm freezing from my mane to my hoof
If I don't get out, I'll freeze or drown
My type aren't meant to swim
We gallop and canter to our heart's content
I slipped and fell with my owner
I don't know where she is.

When I think my time is up
I feel a sharp pull
My body's being lifted up
And pulled towards the ledge
I slip and slide just like before
But this time I have help
I reach the grass and heave myself up
I'm welcomed with towels and blankets
But most of all I'm welcomed by my owner
And she says we're going home.

Eloise Scarborough (11)
Norwich High School for Girls

Fly

I want to be like an eagle
Soaring through the sky,
I want to be free
And I want to fly.
I want to see the mountains
And also the seas,
I also want to explore
Just what I want to be.

I saw an eagle
Fly fadingly into the sun,
That's when I knew
My life had just begun.

Joanna Ellerbrook (12)
Norwich High School for Girls

Proud

You hear about the famous people,
Always looking good,
You hear about how rich they are,
You wonder what it would be like to be famous and cool,
You wonder what it would be like to dress up too.

Your friends could be clever,
Getting straight 'A's,
They're excellent at everything, you know it's true,
Excellent at sport, maths and English too,
Anything they do you think is better than you.

I may not be clever,
Famous too,
I may not have money
Or straight 'A's,
But maybe I have my special ways!

Lottie Wiley (11)
Norwich High School for Girls

Winter

Winter is coming, I can feel the cold air,
Brushing my cheeks and going past my hair,
Making me cold from my fingers to my toes.
Icy roads you'd better watch out,
Making you slip all about.
Try not to skid,
You might hit a kid.
Snow is falling thick and fast,
Icy frostbite on the grass.
Snowball fights in the snow,
One just hit my toe.
The children out in the streets,
You never know who you could meet.
The snow is melting thick and fast,
There is no longer frostbite on the grass.

Harriet Steggles (12)
Norwich High School for Girls

The Magic Shoes

Dashing, flashing, running fast,
The magic shoes never let you come last,
You win athletics, netball too,
In tests and exams they give you a clue.

Easy peasy done like that,
Homework complete so I can play with my cat,
Tea's all ready, no need to wait,
Straight from the oven onto the plate.

My bed's not used, no sleeping done,
I watch TV and have some fun,
Nights go by and mornings come,
I go to school and suck my thumb.

The work's too easy, that no one knows,
Shoes the secret part of my clothes,
Everybody wears them, but not my sort,
Mine are magical and can't be bought.

Abigail Grattan (11)
Norwich High School for Girls

Alone

I sit and stare but there's no one there, no one there at all,
No one there to hear me scream as I fall and fall and fall,
No one there to pull me up and save me from my fate,
No one there to stop them charging at me from every side,
No one there to stop them harming and ruining someone's life,
No one there to help me when I most need someone by my side,
No one around to hear me scream in pain and agony,
No one there to heal my wounds physically and mentally,
No one there to say to me, 'It's OK, everything will be fine.'
No one there that I can trust and know that they'll always be there,
No one there to hold me close and keep me warm in the cold rain,
No one there to say, 'I love you,' just no one there at all,
I sit and stare but there's no one there, no one there at all.

Victoria Weal (13)
Norwich High School for Girls

Enchantment

Enchantment is the star speckled sky,
when you gaze into nothingness and wonder.

Enchantment is the sound of leaves rustling,
breezes blowing and bees humming.

Enchantment is beauty, grace and imagination,
flavoured with moonbeams.

Enchantment has a face,
the face of a laughing child, pure and harmless.

Enchantment smells like freshly-cut grass,
wood smoke, the garden after rain.

It's here, there and everywhere,
it's where you are, have been and will be.

Enchantment is whatever you want it to be.

Camilla Chenery (14)
Norwich High School for Girls

Swimming

I love swimming, I feel fast and strong
I feel like I should never stop and always go on
I love the feeling when you get out of school
And jump into a nice refreshing pool
When I swim, I feel like a mermaid
With a big fin, that's why I love swimming.

Victoria Helman (11)
Norwich High School for Girls

Seasons

Have you ever dwelled on the thought,
Wondered how seasons blend into one another,
How they morph - like a butterfly's wing?

Every season leaves a spark behind
And every season is of colour
And spectacular dances.

The trees bare - or laden,
Move in a swaying dance,
Swinging amongst the everlasting seasons.

And as we affect the colours of the sky,
With our enchanting emotions,
We see . . .

Ruby, violet, pink, every colour,
Flashing past our eyes -
Perfectly innocent.

Faérea Langridge (11)
Norwich High School for Girls

Unhappily Happy

Emotions run high,
All my feelings turn into actions,
I shout and shout until I can't shout anymore,
I can't think straight,
My eyes fill with tears and I cry, cry, cry,
What's the point of living I think to myself,
I might as well be dead
And what's all these emotions, thoughts and actions
Coming out for?
They're coming out for love!

Jade Hardesty (13)
Reepham High School

Remember?

Why?
Why now?
Why have you left me?
I am all alone now, I have no one.
You were my only friend and now you are gone.
I remember the way the wind used to whip my hair around my face as we rode along the open hillside.
I remember your warm, steady heartbeat when I held you close.
I remember the feeling of joy as I touched your delicate, soft body.
I remember we were so strong together, we could conquer anything together.
I remember.
I remember when no one wanted me, you were my friend; you kept me warm at night.
I remember when I broke the ice in winter so you could drink
And I remember you blew down your nose to get my fingers warm.
I remember running beside you as you raced across the vast horizon.
I remember the ground vibrating as you thundered over to greet me.
I remember you rested your head on my shoulder when you were sad.
I remember how you would leap around me when you were happy.
I remember how you would lay so close to me when it was cold.
I remember you taught me to swim in the deep blue river when it was hot, you kept me afloat.
I remember you were the only one for me, you were the special one.

Do you remember?

Hattie Bowden (11)
Reepham High School

The Dragon

The dragon high upon the hill
Many lives it had claimed
Its target was the rotten mill
Where its gold remained

The dwarfs they guarded the mill day and night
Engulfed by fear and fright
That beast, dragon of might
May come down and fight

So the dwarfs they readied themselves
Took axes, swords and halberds from the shelves
They dug great ditches
As to guard their riches

Down the monster came
And the mill was licked in flame
The dwarfs were resilient
And their defence was hell-bent

A chink in his armour they did find
And about this, the dragon was blind
Their crossbows were aimed
And their swords were drawn

Long and hard the battle raged
But the fury of the beast could not be caged
Eventually the dragon fell
Five tolls on the dwavern bell

The dwarfs lived peacefully then on
Repairing the damage that had occurred
After the great battle they had won
And on the monument read only one word
Rest.

Chad Balluza (13)
Reepham High School

My Friend - To Hanag luv Atel

A friend is someone you can trust,
Someone whose shoulder you can cry on,
Someone you can always turn to.

A friend is a part of your life, a part of you,
Someone who understands,
Someone who needs no words to know that you love them.

A friend is someone you can share everything with,
Someone who can comprehend your nonsense,
Someone who can make nonsense of their own.

A friend is your rival, your inspiration and your victory,
Someone who you work hard for,
Someone who is there to comfort you.

You never quite know how much that friend means to you,
Until they're gone.
Over a distance the friendship may be different,
They may not be there for you always,
To provide a shoulder to cry on,
To comfort you when you need comforting.

But I will forever keep a place in my heart for my friend
And a warm seat in my life where she will always be welcome,
For she is a part of me and I love her
And she loves me too.

Sofii Payne (14)
Reepham High School

I Look Up To You

I watch the spirals; grey and dull,
Twisting above and below my feet.
I sink, alone, through mists of despair,
Losing my grip on humanity.

The crowded rooms are forgotten and gone,
Above my head, they spin softly away,
I hit rock bottom, rock solid bottom,
I have lost my grip.

Death looks good from down here,
I never meant to drag you down but,
I was just searching for a ladder,
Wow, death looks good from down here.

The monsters plague my sleep,
The days are restless treacheries,
I can't stand to be alone,
But alone is the best place to stand.

The rising sun; I see no light,
The monsters cross to day from night,
I can't believe my eyes.

Death looks good from down here.

Sian Hamer (14)
Reepham High School

Living In The Country

Living in the country,
Happy sun,
Warm me,
Rustling leaves,
Shade me,
Lonely leaves,
Follow me,
Chilly wind,
Cool me,
Summer sun, sparkling,
In the running water,
Wavy grass,
Tickle me,
Living in the country.

Liberty Smith (13)
Reepham High School

Guess My Name?

My wing's a net of glittery feathers,
My skin soft velvet that I am wrapped in
My shoes hard as rock that shall not break
My neck a purple arm rest

My home, the clouds, a puff of smoke
The ground is where I lay, where my children play near
The rainbow we seek where we are coloured
The water I drink through my white pearly teeth

My horn a glittery, galaxy-coloured within

So guess my name or read the clues again.

Zoe Goff (13)
Reepham High School

Apocalypse

What have I become?
I am nothing,
Tied to machines,
Oh to die,
Oh to be free.

I cannot live,
I cannot die,
I cannot be
Stuck for eternity.

Still alive,
In an empty shell,
Pulsating brain,
I cannot describe the pain.

Death,
War,
Famine,
Pestilence,
I've seen them all
And suffered from them too.

I cannot live,
It must end,
It is my time
And your time too.

As fire drops like rain,
As the seas boil as if the Earth is a kettle,
The Earth cracks like the shell of a nut,
Leaving us to pay for our sins.

Kevin Ryan (13)
Reepham High School

Living?

A mottled green hand comes out of the almost black shadows,
Searching for what it cannot believe,
Crawling and sliding along the sewage-covered path,
Seeing what it cannot see.

Brown rotting legs now emerge from the darkness,
Being dragged raw by the crawling soul,
The faceless being stops, then peers through the gloom,
Thick, grey fog is the sight the creature sees.

A scythe, long and ancient, lies in the path,
The old centuries and new months have cursed it,
Rusty and old, it blocks the creature's path,
Changed in the winds means nothing,
But the creature sees what cannot be seen.

Life is no longer a light in most,
But this is the last being with it.

Jack Churchill (13)
Reepham High School

Alone

A solitary teardrop runs down her cheek,
like a pebble thrown into the sea, it falls,
lands on the dirty ground
and mixes with the rain.

Pouring down into the dark emptiness,
as if the stars shared her weeping soul.

Misery sunk in as deep as old traditions
flows through her tired heart,
seeps through her blood.

But nobody cares anymore.

Ali Hewson (13)
Reepham High School

My Music

My music is intrinsic to me,
Taking over my mind and body.
Concentrate, focus, keep the rhythm,
Let the dynamics emphasise the beauty of the work.

Do not play for an audience,
Play for self-fulfilment,
Strive for perfection.

Staccato, legato, tumbling triplets,
Dance in waves of crescendos.
Vivace, diminuendos into a largo tempo,
Little droplets of perspiration puncture my skin.

Keep the concentration,
Count the beats,
Keep the tempo,
Gracefully chase those dynamics,
To the final crescendoing fortissimo.

Receive the applause with relief,
Pride and knowledge of a piece
Engendered centuries ago has
Come to life once again.

Philippa Briggs (13)
Reepham High School

Walking Away Personification

As I walk away the trees are waving to me,
As I walk away leaves are surfing down from trees,
As I walk away the sun is smiling at me,
As I walk away the benches say *come sit down on me*,
When I turn away it turns silent.

Zoë Allen (11)
Reepham High School

View From The Window

Like a drop of ink onto a wet piece of paper,
It grows and grows,
Like a cancer to the soul,
Exceeding its own grit and grime and grey,
To the yet unspoilt, surrounding countryside,
Engulfing every slither of grass and another,
Ocean-blue horizon,
Suffocated, without the blink of an eye.

Sculpturing the landscape like a soft lump of clay,
Hasty and spinning in a continual whirl
Of steamy, greedy selfishness,
No time to turn,
To look and see what it has done,
What we have done,
Handing out orders to Mother Nature,
Changing the way she leads her life.

Only when the rays of sunshine leave us,
Only after the last leaf, of the last tree falls
And our last hope drowns,
Will we realise;
We are powerless without the solitary silence
Of the coloured portrait we see,
When we look out of the window.

Rosie Crawley (14)
Reepham High School

Beyond The Mirage

Please stop pushing me,
From all around me it drips,
Sour liquor leaks into my carcass.
The fatal blow is dealt.
It claws to my heart.

Fiery forked tongues lick at my cracked face,
My spirit streaks away.
Please say I've one too many beers again.
I peer up.
Light seers at my eyes, I can't close them,
A visage appears.

A light zephyr blows me upward,
I see long-gone faces etched in cloud,
Then I see her.
She smiles and then laughs.

I steadily ascend,
Ouch,
I've hit my head; the ceiling?
I slowly begin to fall towards the floor,
I begin to plummet,
She laughs,
Help!
Clang!

I am on the floor where she left me.
'Hi mate, are you OK?' a voice asks.
I get up, 'Err, yeah. I think so, thanks.'

Edward Jones (13)
Reepham High School

I

I watch
And I see
And I cry

I see the dagger
The torment
The agony
I see the chains

Of nature
And the spirit
And liberation
And all that I believe in

I see the demons of fire
Torrents of blood
And the mushrooms of smoke

I know
All is lost
And all will die

I see man committing suicide
And I am saddened
I see man committing genocide
And I weep

Nothing will last

I was your mother
Your dreams
I was your hope
Your life
I was your beauty
I was

But now
I am the wolf
The storm
I am the death
The chains
I am the dark
I am
Everything you fear

And my tear
Drops into my ocean;
The ripples spread
And disappear

I watch
And I see
And I cry.

Polly Boon (13)
Reepham High School

The Meandering River

The slithering river,
Gently and smoothly it meanders down the valley,
The water crystal clear.

The smell of the storm brewing is arising,
Then suddenly,
It breaks out,
The water is clear no more,
But it becomes a terrifying torrent,
The water is soiled terrain smelling.

The waterfall rages fiercely,
The noise is immense,
Frightening yet exciting.

After a short but shocking moment,
It returns,
To a peaceful picturesque, gently-flowing,
Crystal clear river,
Meandering down the valley.

Leah Perry-Warnes (13)
Reepham High School

Vice Versa

Happiness courses through
  your veins,
Allowing your soul
  to soar.
Everything you feel and touch
  fills you with joy,
It makes you feel content
  and lets your self esteem roar.

Happiness is the wind
  engulfing you,
Letting you scream without
  feeling ashamed.

Depression is imprisonment
Depression is desperation,
It rips your heart;
Eats your mind,
It is a disease,
Which poisons the blood.

It is the look in a dying man's eyes,
When he realises he has never been loved.
Depression prevents laughter
And stimulates loathing,
It smothers your soul;
You can't breathe.

Depression is imprisonment.

Elspeth Clayton (13)
Reepham High School

The Fox And The Chicken

Foxes are all very sly
Once they look their prey in the eye
The fox will crouch down
The chicken will frown

So I leapt to the rescue from high
But before I got there to fight
My chicken gave the fox a big fright
She had trained in kung fu
And was a black belt, it's true

And had chopped him with all of her might
The feathers lay scattered
My chicken was shattered
There were bruises all over his shins

She had mud in her feathers
And had yet to see whether
The fox had escaped past the bins

The fox lay in his big bed
He was glad he was yet to be dead
He was lucky this time to escape
His plan had been foiled
There were potatoes to be boiled
And a measly banana and grape.

Charlie Barnes (11)
Reepham High School

Am I Alone?

I walk through the park day after day,
There's no one around,
I hear leaves rustle,
Am I alone?

I walk down my street night after night,
There's no one in sight,
I see a shadow,
Am I alone?

I walk past my neighbour's door time after time,
The door opens, no one comes out,
I feel someone's here,
Am I alone?

I see shadows,
I hear leaves rustle,
I feel people,
So,
Am I really alone?

Jennifer Boddy (14)
Reepham High School

Sadness

Sadness is a plain, bland white
Sadness smells like a smell that lingers
And tastes like a mouthful of dry biscuits
That you can't swallow
Sadness looks like a small animal
Lonely and separated from its mother
Whimpering in the darkness
Sadness sounds like an ongoing buzz
And feels like a large rock in the pit of your stomach.

Ellen Goodby (12)
Reepham High School

My Christmas Day

On Christmas Day in the morning
Everyone is full of excitement
After our breakfast of chilled champagne and smoked salmon
We begin to open our presents
Around the crackling fire we open our gifts in wonder
Thank yous and *you're welcomes* are repeatedly replied
This is my Christmas day

On Christmas Day in the afternoon
The sweet smell of roast beef and potatoes fill the house
As does the gentle carollers' singing
And laughter of the family
Each present is enjoyed, appreciated
And shared with one another
This is my Christmas Day

On Christmas Day in the evening
Everyone is sleepy-eyed and their bellies are full
Decorations are drooping
And the champagne is all gone
The day is over
This was my Christmas Day.

Alice Butler (13)
Reepham High School

Life

We have had laughs and we have had cries,
As we watch the world go whizzing by,
We think and wonder what the world was like,
When we had no transport but just a bike,
I got up early and worked till dawn,
I then got home and cut the lawn,
We have had no family,
It's just been us: her and me.

Andrew Harding (12)
Reepham High School

A 1951 Television

A 1951 television,
Only colours,
Black and white,
Blinking pinpricks of light,
No colour.

A television fails,
Is replaced,
Colour fills the screen.

A bright sphere,
A blue-green ball,
Full of seething life,
Only satellites know,
The pure beauty.

A 1951 television,
Only colours,
Black and white,
Blinking pinpricks of light,
Full of colour and life.

Hugh Derry (14)
Reepham High School

Life

The old life goes sailing down the river,
The old farmer and his wife work slowly in the field,
The old hut stands firm on the mountain,
They sit calmly outside,
They talk quietly and slowly.

Michael Lawson (12)
Reepham High School

The Shy One

Maybe you don't know her,
Maybe you never will,
But when you see her there,
All alone, you'll know who she is,
The shy one.

A brain so willing,
Yet a heart so lonesome,
A quick lip,
A quiet soul,
But when you meet her,
Maybe once, you'll know who she is,
The shy one.

No one sees her true shape,
For it is hidden, deep below,
But when you spot her,
The hurt heart,
You'll know who she is,
The shy one.

Anna Husbands (13)
Reepham High School

The Gale!

The wind is howling in my ears,
Through my hair and touching my tears.
The trees are swaying, quietly praying,
Whispering about the old trees saying,
'The years to come, the years that were,
The years that could have been.'

Anna Clough (11)
Reepham High School

Object In The Background

Swishing, swaying, listen in the background,
Rustling, green, distorted shapes,
Sometimes they change colours to match their mood,
Look out the window,
In the morning, you see what it is,
But at night they are strange, mysterious and scary things
You can sometimes see an old woman or man
Withering away in the middle of this monstrosity,
Children always play on these wonderful creations,
Without considering the beauty of it,
Crunching, crunching under your feet,
The fingers of this big monstrosity snap off the hands,
As the day comes you can see clearly what they are,
They are wonderful, beautiful trees.

Elizabeth Barnes (13)
Reepham High School

The Wilderness Inside Me

There is a kangaroo jumping inside me
Leaping around happily.

There is a wasp inside me, stirring up my anger
Stinging those in my way.

There is a dog inside me who comforts me when I am sad
Laying his head on my knee.

There is a tortoise inside me, to steal my laziness
Stopping me from lying around.

There is a greyhound inside me for sportiness and freedom
Running without a lead.

There is a squirrel inside me, squeaking with fear
Hiding and scratching up a tree.

Karen Harding (11)
Reepham High School

Widow

I stand in the coldness of the corner of the room
I will always wear black now
To remember him
To remember my love

Every day I weep, just wishing
I had one more chance to put things right
My friends try to comfort me
But I can never forget
I can never forget that dreadful night
When my love died

It was all so sudden
The crash that claimed his life
I know there was nothing I could do
But I can't help to feel responsible for his death

I try to move on
Forget the past
But I can never forget my love
I could never love another
I am a widow and I will always be one.

Lewis Rayner (13)
Reepham High School

The Old Couple

They've been there for each other
Ever since I can remember
They have always been happy
They always loved the children of the town
But never had the chance to have their own
But all of that has changed now
Now that she is dead, he isn't happy anymore
He just sits there
I guess wishing his life would end
It will; one day.

Katie Robertson (12)
Reepham High School

My Faithful Companion

When I awake early every day,
She is there to greet me in her joyous way,
The bang, banging of her wagging tail upon the kitchen door,
Shows she cannot hide her excitement no more,
I stroke her golden long soft hair,
As when she is near there is nothing to fear.
When I gaze into her big brown eyes,
My love for her replies,
Her long pink tongue gives me a comforting lick,
During those times when I am feeling sick.
In the spring breeze her hair will blow,
Such a loyal dog keeps my spirits up when I am feeling low.
When I return home from school there she sits by the old rusted gate,
Patiently waiting even when I am late.
On our walk we run through fields, streams and brier
And come home to lie together beside the fire,
Oh it is such a delight,
To fall asleep beside my faithful dog each night.
I know one day she won't be here,
The thought of this reduces me to a tear,
But the memories she leaves behind are all mine
And maybe my heart will mend over time.

Claire Hudson (14)
Reepham High School

Fight Of Wits

In a field there is a battle of wits and death,
What will become of me?
Will I rot like my friends or will I be hit by a flying bullet or bomb?
What is happening to my family?
Are they dead or are they alive and well?
Every day I smell and taste blood in the air.
Will it ever go away?
Head in my hands crying, I pray to God.
Will it ever stop? Will we win or will we lose?

Thomas Gayler (11)
Reepham High School

Midnight

Midnight, midnight, it's as dark as it can be,
it's not the place where you should be,
it's not the place for you and me.

So get home quick,
it's far too late
and stay home in the warm, warm, warm.

Midnight, midnight, where foxes crawl,
waiting to catch their prey,
I'm glad I have a place to stay.

Midnight, midnight, wind is calm,
there's no one in sight
apart from the stray cats having a fight.

So get home quick,
it's far too late
and stay home in the warm, warm, warm.

Midnight, midnight, nothing but pitch-black,
so go home and don't play with midnight.

Georgie Harrington (11)
Reepham High School

Dying

Sitting on the porch with his wife
carving the stick with his knife

His wife sitting with him close and snug
but this is the last time they'll have a hug

One of these days she'll pass away
on his own he'll watch the trees sway

But now he's making the most of it
although there's no stopping those frequent fits

The day has arrived, now's the time for Ethel to pass away
Eddie's going to miss her day by day.

Stuart Brookshaw (12)
Reepham High School

The Song Of The Birds

The singing of the robin,
the cooing of the dove,
the screeching of the little owl,
fills me full of love.

The warble of the kingfisher,
the harsh call of the jay,
the chatter of the magpie,
can get me through all day.

The tinkling of the goldfinch,
the screaming of the swift,
the trill of the blue tit,
can give the day a lift.

The song of the birds in the morning,
prepares me for all day,
they sing on all through winter,
March, April and May.

Kirsty Saker (12)
Reepham High School

The Daisy

The daisy's beaming yellow face,
Peeps over the towering emerald green grass,
Standing proudly,
Her delicate features admire the glistening sun,
Dancing through the entwining foliage,
Reaching out to neighbouring weeds for balance,
Her petals like silken strands,
Ripple in the breeze
And clad in leafy green,
Fit to be the belle of any ball.

Vita Sunter (12)
Reepham High School

My Friend, Jack

Ponies are small, round and fat,
Every time they're good they get a pat.
Horses are bigger, more elegant and bright,
Some of them grow to quite a height.
Most are greedy and will do anything for food,
If deprived of oats they get in quite a mood,
But over the years I've grown quite attached,
To a particular horse that's easy to catch.
He's loving and soft, gentle and kind,
He's never ever left me behind.
Once beautiful and shiny, colourful and light,
Now he is old and not so right,
But his eyes light up as I come down to the stable,
Tack him up, strong and able.
As we trot up the road, we look quite a pair,
He's happy, content and has lost his despair.
As I drink my tea, I look out to the meadows
And see him dancing free of shadows.

Rebecca Caine (12)
Reepham High School

The Decaying Tree

The decaying tree stands alone
Its branches reaching to the sky
In mid-winter
The decaying tree has no leaves

The decaying tree stands alone
Its gnarled, twisted branches reaching to the icy clouds
Orange fungi grow near the base
Crumpled and shrivelled with age

Dead branches, rusting like old iron
Reach towards the icy-blue moon
The decaying tree has stood there for many centuries
And it will stand there for many more.

Guy Jackson (11)
Reepham High School

Time

Time to come
Time to go
Time is all we need

Time for this
Time for that
Time is all we need

Time for cooking
Time for cleaning
Time is all we need

Time for moving
Time for thinking
Time is all we need

Time is testing
Time is useful
Time is all we need

Time for me
Time for you
Time is all we need

Time for school
Time for play
Time is all we need

Time for lunch
Time for tea
Time is all we need

Time for action
Time to be awake
Time is all we need

Time is ticking
Time has nearly gone
Time is all we need

Time for teeth
Time for hair
Time is all we need

Time for bed
Time to sleep
Time is all we need.

Alice Court (11)
Reepham High School

Someone Special

Someone special was here today
Then one day they went away
Someday I'll find that special person
I don't know how and I don't know when
So I'll be sitting in my little den

Someone special was here today
Then one day they just went away
I'm still thinking
And my eyes are blinking
How many years will pass
And I'll be lying in a bed of grass

Someone special was here today
Then one day they just went away
I'm really missing that person
Someday I'll find that special someone
But until then I'll be thinking.

Nikita Williamson (12)
Reepham High School

Yesterday

Yesterday, yesterday, yesterday,
Why do I keep thinking about yesterday?
Maybe it's because of all the memories
Or maybe it's because of all the things that happened,
No, I know why, it's because of my dear old grandparents.

Yesterday is when I was drinking milk with them and eating cookies,
Yesterday is when they kissed me goodnight.

Yesterday Grandad was cleaning out the barn in his old dungarees,
He uses a pitchfork which has been engraved with the words
I will love you forever, which Nanny did with an old rusty knife.

Yesterday is when Nanny was knitting me a jumper
With the wool from one of her sheep,
She only has 5 sheep so I was privileged.

Yesterday is when they spent their last day together,
Yesterday is when their life ended,
Yesterday is when we all said our goodbyes,
Yesterday is when they had gone forever,
Why do I keep thinking about yesterday?
Yesterday, yesterday, yesterday.

Lucy Cook (12)
Reepham High School

The Thing From Below

Its demon eyes glow red with fire,
Its claws curl up with so much power.
Its back hunched up ready to pounce,
With all its weight, not leaving an ounce.

He waits in the shadows,
For when he's going to strike,
For if you are near,
Tremble with fear,
For nothing can leave its sight.

Matthew Fletcher (13)
Reepham High School

My Dream Pony

My perfect pony would be clever and bright,
Growing and growing to a huge height.
He'd come to the fence when it's time to go in,
Knowing that when he was in, it would be time for din-dins.
He'd be easy to ride and delightful to know,
Every time he was entered, he'd win his show.
He would be so soft, gentle and kind,
Never once kicking me from behind.
He would never get dirty and always look his best,
He would solve every problem and pass every test.
He'd be so fit and agile and jump like a flea,
But all the time looking happy and pleased.
This would not happen and it's all a dream,
I'm not sure I would be this keen.
My little Shetland will do me just fine,
Well maybe for now, but not in a little while.

Polly Egmore (12)
Reepham High School

The Ghost Picture

Taking the picture of the barn,
There's no one there,
But when I get them developed,
I see them, just like you do.
Why are they there?
It's my grandad on the left,
With my gran on the right,
So I go back,
Take it again.
I get them developed,
They've gone - disappeared again,
Did we imagine it
Or were they really there?

Georgina Hardiment (12)
Reepham High School

The Troll

Be wary of the scary troll
That quietly lies in wait
To drag you to his dingy hole
To put you on his plate

His blood is green and scorching hot
He growls, grizzles and groans
Ready to push you in his dinner pot
Your skin, your flesh, your bones

He'll twist your arms and grate your legs
And crush you to a pulp
Then swallow you like a big mouth frog
Golly, golly, gulp!

So watch your step when next you go
Upon a lovely stroll
Or you might end in the hole below
As lunch for the ugly *troll!*

Rebecca Dawson-Tuck (12)
Reepham High School

The Screamer

Round and round goes the Catherine wheel
Bang! Up goes the rocket
Crackle, crackle the bonfire goes
No fireworks in my pocket

The loudest firework of them all
Is my favourite called the screamer!
When it goes up in the air
It explodes just like a streamer

The fireworks light up the sky
In red, blue, gold and green
The sight of all the fireworks
Are the best I've ever seen!

Rachael Sarsby (11)
Reepham High School

The Unicorn

Her sleek, shimmering waterfall of hair cascades about her shoulders,
Her horn, infinitely dangerous and sharp as a hidden thief's
dirk, awaits foolish confront,
Her pearly tail billows in the night breeze, an artful tumble of
molten silver.
Her hooves silently tread the grass, studded by gems of dew,
leaving no vestige of her passing,
Her powerful shoulders and smooth, muscular flanks
proclaim her Queen,
Her very presence is an exquisite, excited whisper of the night.
Her dark, bottomless eyes gleam brightly, her shrewd intelligence
evident, as she watches and she waits for the silver goddess of
the sky, round and full, to manifest Herself,
Casting long shadows on the ground, illuminating the stark beauty
of the unicorn.
She has not a care in the world as she doth wait for the true beauty
of the night to awake,
For the tall, lush trees to wave and rustle, while the crickets
pipe and sing
And the plants of colour bow to the many sparkling princesses
of above in this nightly waltz.
Yet when the unicorn hears a tear in the night's fabric of silence,
She waits still, letting the voices of men come nearer.
She knows they carry black tubes of sound, yet she stands in her
effortless sanguine grace, regarding the rustling trees.
As the hunters emerge, her eyes meet the men's and sudden
understanding floods her in a torrent of fear.
The sickening knowledge that she has watched too long strikes deep
in her heart as she swiftly turns to run.

And falls in her step,
To the sound of a gun.

Rachel Staddon (14)
Reepham High School

Autumn

Autumn's here,
No more summer,
Bare trees,
Sun on fire.

Wind blows,
Trees sway,
Golden leaves
And a sunlight ray.

Leaves falling,
To and fro,
Flowers gone,
Temperatures low.

Mist in the morning,
Cold and nippy,
Leaves on the pavement,
Wet and slippy.

Red lemon leaves,
Softly float down,
The sun sets,
Like a golden crown.

Insects gone,
Birds are hiding,
No more creatures,
Badgers sleeping.

Shorter days,
Winter's calling,
Fires crackle,
Cold is coming.

Hannah Vogler
Reepham High School

Guilt

The light of the lamp posts glared down at me
As they started their interrogation on me
About what I had done.
As I walked down the alleyway,
Trying to hide my guilt,
I could not stand the eyes of the broken glass
As I stared at it.
I tried to keep a low profile,
But the telephone box wouldn't stop
Its horrid ringing as it bellowed its accusations
Into my ear as if it knew what I had done.

Oliver Mellish (11)
Reepham High School

Up In The Mountains

Up in the mountains you'll always find rain
Breaking through the rocks to form a stream
Trickling down the rocky cliff
To where low cloud looks like misty steam

Up in the mountains the air is so clean
With no foul smoke or dirty fumes
Where mountain climbers fulfil their dreams
Where creatures can be free and know no threat

Up in the mountains there is no hurry
There is no worry and there is no time
Some people go for the beautiful view
While others like the stress of the climb

Up in the mountains the sights are sublime
The sheep try to hide in the bushes and grass
Most people don't even notice a sign
Of the harmless animals waiting for peace.

Stuart Feek (14)
The Blyth-Jex School

The Fox

I am the fox,
The silent wanderer;
I walk alone.
The thinker and philosopher,
Unwelcome, an outcast,
But I do not moan.

I see,
I listen,
But what I know I do not share,
For who with, who can I tell?
There are no other foxes here.

Underestimated and hated,
Make no enemy of this warrior;
She will not be baited.
Cunning, quick and clever,
The lone warrior,
She gives up never!

Brave fighter and true to the end,
The only thing this fox cries for is a friend.

Carolyn Hylton (15)
The Blyth-Jex School

Autumn Leaves

Leaves are falling out of trees
Leaves are falling at your knees
Leaves are falling all so bright
Wet and shiny in the night.

Sarah Hawkins (12)
The Blyth-Jex School